Loch Ness *and the* North East Highlands

W A L K S

Compiled by
Neil Wilson

JARROLD

Ordnance Survey

Acknowledgements
I would like to thank the following people for their help in the preparation of this guide: Janet Clark at the Scottish Rights of Way Society; Kevin Peace, Moira Baptie and Malcolm Wield of Forest Enterprise; Graham Smith and Denise Strang at the Highlands of Scotland Tourist Board; and the many local people who offered advice and directions. Thanks also to Moira MacDonald for providing accommodation in Brora, and to Carol Downie and Fiona McIntyre for help with transport arrangements.

Text:	Neil Wilson
Photography:	Neil Wilson
Editors:	Thomas Albrighton, Julie Beesley, Richard Crowest
Designers:	Brian Skinner, Doug Whitworth
Mapping:	Heather Pearson, Tina Shaw

Series Consultant: Brian Conduit

© Jarrold Publishing and Ordnance Survey 1998
Maps © Crown copyright 1998. The mapping in this guide is based upon Ordnance Survey ® Pathfinder ®, Outdoor Leisure ™, Explorer ™ and Travelmaster ® mapping.
Ordnance Survey, Pathfinder and Travelmaster are registered trade marks and Outdoor Leisure and Explorer are trade marks of Ordnance Survey, the National Mapping Agency of Great Britain.

Jarrold Publishing   ISBN 0-7117-0991-2

First published 1998
by Jarrold Publishing and Ordnance Survey
Printed in Great Britain
by Jarrold Book Printing, Thetford 1/98

Jarrold Publishing,
Whitefriars, Norwich NR3 1TR
Ordnance Survey,
Romsey Road, Southampton SO16 4GU

Front cover:	Inverness Castle
Previous page:	The Geo of Sclaites, Duncansby Head

Contents

■ Short, easy walks

■ Walks of modest length, likely to involve some modest uphill walking

■ More challenging walks which may be longer and/or over more rugged terrain, often with some stiff climbs

SCALE 1:384 615 or 1 INCH to about 6 MILES *1CM to 3.8KM*

0   2   4   6   8   10 KILOMETRES 15

0   2   4   6   MILES 8   10

KEYMAP HEIGHTS SHOWN IN FEET

SCALE 1:384 615 or 1 INCH to about 6 MILES *1CM to 3.8KM*

0 2 4 6 8 10 KILOMETRES 15

0 2 4 6 MILES 8 10

KEYMAP HEIGHTS SHOWN IN FEET

Keymap 3

Keymap 3

Walk	Page	Start	Distance	Time	Highest Point
Ben Griam Beg	71	North of Kinbrace, Sutherland, on A897	9 miles (14.5km)	5 hrs	1902ft (580m)
Ben Klibreck	83	Near Altnaharra, on A836	7 miles (11.3km)	5 hrs	3153ft (961m)
Ben Rinnes	66	South-west of Dufftown	4½ miles (7.2km)	3 hrs	2756ft (840m)
Ben Wyvis	80	Garbat, Easter Ross, on the A835	8 miles (12.9km)	5 hrs	3432ft (1046m)
Big Burn Glen and Ben Bhraggie	57	Near Golspie, Sutherland	6 miles (9.7km)	3 hrs	1300ft (396m)
The Black Rock of Novar	24	Evanton, Easter Ross	2½ miles (4km)	1½ hrs	330ft (100m)
Brora to Carn Liath Broch	32	Brora, Sutherland	8½ miles (13.7km)	4 hrs	33ft (10m)
Carbisdale Wood	28	Culrain, near Bonar Bridge, Easter Ross	2½ miles (4km)	2 hrs	400ft (122m)
Chanonry Point and the Fairy Glen	39	Rosemarkie, Easter Ross	7 miles (11.3km)	3½ hrs	460ft (140m)
Covesea Coast	45	Hopeman, near Elgin	8½ miles (13.7km)	4 hrs	100ft (30m)
Craig Phadrig	18	Leachkin Brae, Inverness	2 miles (3.2km)	1 hr	564ft (172m)
Culbin Forest	53	Wellfill car park, near Forres	8½ miles (13.7km)	4 hrs	100ft (30m)
Farigaig Forest	42	Inverfarigaig, Loch Ness	5½ miles (8.9km)	3 hrs	660ft (201m)
Findhorn Gorge	26	South of Forres, on A940	2½ miles (4km)	1½ hrs	360ft (110m)
The Glen Loth Hills	74	Near Brora, Sutherland	6½ miles (10.5km)	4 hrs	2045ft (623m)
Knock Farril and Cnoc Mor	36	Strathpeffer, Easter Ross	4½ miles (7.2km)	2½ hrs	882ft (269m)
Loch Affric	68	River Affric car park, west of Cannich	11 miles (17.7km)	5½ hrs	1082ft (330m)
Meallfuarvonie	64	Near Drumnadrochit, Loch Ness	6 miles (9.7km)	3 hrs	2293ft (699m)
Morven	77	Braemore, near Dunbeath, Caithness	10 miles (16.1km)	6 hrs	2316ft (706m)
Ness Islands and Tomnahuirich	22	Whin Park, Inverness	4½ miles (7.2km)	2½ hrs	230ft (70m)
Noss Head	34	Staxigoe, near Wick	5½ miles (8.9km)	2½ hrs	130ft (40m)
River Oich	20	On Auchtsraw road near Fort Augustus	4 miles (6.4km)	2 hrs	100ft (30m)
Rogie Falls and the View Rock	30	Near Contin, Easter Ross	5 miles (8km)	3 hrs	530ft (161m)
The Speyside Way	50	Spey Bay, near Fochabers	10 miles (16.1km)	4 hrs	110ft (34m)
The Stacks of Duncansby	16	Duncansby Head car park, near John o' Groats	2 miles (3.2km)	1 hr	215ft (65m)
Struie Hill	48	West of Tain, Easter Ross	4 miles (6.4km)	2½ hrs	1217ft (371m)
Tarbat Ness and Portmahomack	60	Tarbat Ness, east of Tain, Easter Ross	8½ miles (13.7km)	4 hrs	100ft (30m)
Wade's Road to the Corrieyairack Pass	86	Near Fort Augustus	14 miles (22.5km)	7 hrs	2552ft (778m)

Comments

A lonely peak topped by Scotland's highest hill fort. The long approach, rough walking and remote location mean that this hill, though small, should not be undertaken lightly.

This remote Munro in central Sutherland provides a magnificent viewpoint. The ascent is steep and strenuous, and full hill-walking gear will be required.

The granite tors of the summit command a sweeping panorama extending from the Cairngorms to the Moray Firth. Nearby whisky distilleries are an added attraction.

The highest summit in this guide, Ben Wyvis is a haven for alpine flora and mountain birds such as ptarmigan and dotterel. Summit conditions can be cold and windy, even in summer.

A towering monument to the Duke of Sutherland makes Ben Bhraggie a prominent local landmark. This walk takes the long but easy route up the back of the hill.

Glacial meltwaters cut deep into the bedrock to create this remarkable gorge. A short walk through pleasant woodland leads to two footbridges over the spectacular ravine.

Coastal wildlife, beautiful views, and an Iron Age broch add interest to an enjoyable excursion along the Sutherland shore. Easy walking, suitable for young children.

A short hike through the forest leads to a pretty loch with a picnic site, then continues to the site of a historic battle. Nearby Carbisdale Castle is worth a look in passing.

Bring your binoculars, as this walk takes in a favourite dolphin-watching site. Coast and hill are combined in one walk, or can be enjoyed separately on different days.

A smuggler's coast, riddled with caves, stretches east from the harbour at Hopeman. This walk explores the cliff-tops, then returns by way of the famous Gordonstoun School.

This little, wooded hill, crowned by a vitrified Iron Age fort, overlooks Inverness and the Beauly Firth. A short and not too strenuous climb.

A long but varied expedition that takes in Culbin Forest, Findhorn Bay and the beaches of the nearby coast. Sound navigation is needed to negotiate the maze of forest tracks.

A brisk climb through forestry plantations, with fine views over Loch Ness, leads to a pretty lochan, while the return leg descends through attractive native woodland.

Beautiful woods surround this scenic stretch of the River Findhorn, where a cliff-top path offers dizzying views into a deep, rock-bound gorge.

The heather-clad hills above lonely Glen Loth enjoy a real sense of isolation, while offering grand views over the Moray Firth. Access restricted during the stalking season.

These diminutive summits overlooking Strathpeffer offer delightful walking, with grand views across the strath to the looming bulk of Ben Wyvis.

A long but level hike on good paths that leads deep into the heart of the mountains, and reveals some of Scotland's most magnificent scenery.

This rounded hill is easily overlooked, but provides the best viewpoint in the Great Glen. The walking is fairly easy, but map and compass should be carried in case of bad weather.

The ascent of this remote but shapely hill involves a long, rough approach and a hard, tiring grind up loose scree, but the magnificent views and splendid isolation are well worth it.

This urban walk manages to squeeze a lot into a relatively short distance – river, islands, woods, hilltop and canal bank. Particularly recommended on a sunny, summer evening.

A walk through classic Caithness scenery of level farmland fringed by flagstone sea-cliffs leads to an atmospheric ruined castle perched dramatically atop a sea-girt crag.

A relaxing stroll amid woods and wild flowers on the banks of the pretty River Oich. Bring along a packed lunch and take advantage of a beautiful riverside picnic spot.

Watch for salmon leaping the falls at the renowned beauty spot of Rogie Falls before climbing to the Victorian lookout of View Rock. Easy walking on forest trails.

This route follows the first few miles of the Speyside Way long-distance footpath before returning along a quiet back-road and crossing a splendid 19th-century railway viaduct.

A short and easy walk to view some of the most spectacular coastal scenery on Scotland's eastern seaboard. The cliffs here are also an excellent venue for bird-watching.

The long ridge of Struie Hill is a fine viewpoint overlooking the Kyle of Sutherland. The high starting point makes for a short and easy climb to the summit.

This long, circular route takes in both sides of the narrow Tarbat peninsula, with the pretty village of Portmahomack providing a convenient break at the halfway mark.

The return trip along the old military road to the summit of the Corrieyairack Pass is hard on the feet, but the effort is rewarded with fine views and a real sense of history.

Introduction to Inverness, Loch Ness and the North East Highlands

The area covered by this guide is centred on the Highland 'capital' of Inverness, and extends north and east along the shores of the Moray Firth, and south and west to Fort Augustus and Glen Affric, encompassing Caithness, eastern Sutherland, Easter Ross, the Black Isle, Moray, and the banks of Loch Ness.

The North East Highlands have a distinctive character that is very different to the rugged wilderness of the west coast with its scattered jigsaw of islands, ragged sea-lochs and bare, rocky mountains. Here a patchwork quilt of fertile farmland lines the shores of the Moray Firth, and the heather-clad hills are lower and more rounded. The climate is softer too, lying in the rain-shadow of the Highlands and protected from the prevailing south-westerly winds – Nairn is one of the driest and sunniest places in Scotland.

For the walker, the region's attractions are many and varied, from the wild and lonely hills of Sutherland and the sea-cliffs of Caithness, to Glen Affric's native pine woods and Moray's magnificent salmon rivers. There is the added bonus that the North East Highlands are far less busy than the popular walking areas of the Cairngorms, Glencoe and Torridon, and it is quite common to have a hilltop or beach all to yourself.

Geology and scenery

Much of the area around the shores of the Moray Firth is underlain by reddish-brown sandstones and conglomerates that are commonly referred to as the 'Old Red Sandstone', a name given to them by geologists in the early 19th century. These rocks were laid down during the Devonian period (between 360 and 400 million years ago), and are composed of sediments – pebbles, gravel, sand and silt – that were eroded from ancient mountain ranges and deposited in alluvial fans, rivers and lakes.

The coarsest sediments were compacted to form a rock called conglomerate, in which boulders and pebbles of granite, quartzite and schist reveal the rock types of which the ancient mountains were composed. These conglomerates have proved more resistant to recent erosion than the surrounding rocks, and now form many of the prominent summits around the Moray Firth, including Morven, Ben Bhraggie, Struie Hill, Knock Farril, View Rock, Craig Phadrig and Meallfuarvonie.

Finer-grained sediments were deposited in a huge lake which once covered the area now occupied by Caithness and Orkney, and these became the thin-bedded grey flagstones that have been extensively quarried in the past for roofing slates and paving slabs, and that contain the famous Old Red Sandstone 'fish beds' – rich fossil deposits that were described in detail by local geologist Hugh Miller of Cromarty in the 19th century. The flagstones are responsible for the distinctive Caithness scenery of undulating

Elegant suspension footbridges span the River Ness at Inverness

lowland and dramatic, stratified sea-cliffs riven by 'geos' – sheer-sided clefts that have been eroded along lines of weakness in the flagstone beds.

Further inland, the basement rocks which underlie the Old Red Sandstone sediments are exposed. These consist of metamorphic schists, gneisses and quartzites collectively known as the 'Moine Schist', which can be seen in the rocky outcrops of Ben Wyvis, Ben Klibreck, the Corrieyairack Pass and Glen Affric. Ben Rinnes, to the south of the Moray Firth, is composed of granite.

Wildlife and vegetation

Beyond the farmland of the coastal fringes, the characteristic vegetation of the North East Highlands is the heather moor, which persists up to an altitude of around 2500ft (762m), above which a sparse, sub-arctic community of grasses, mosses, and rare alpine plants takes over. Ben Wyvis in particular is known for its alpine flora. These airy heights are home to mountain birds such as ptarmigan and dotterel, and the majestic golden eagle whose chief prey, the mountain hare, can occasionally be seen bounding through the heather. Both hare and ptarmigan moult in spring and autumn, exchanging their drab summer colours for a winter coat of dazzling white.

The Highland glens were once covered in forests of Scots pine, birch and alder, but very little of this native woodland now remains. One of the largest remnants is found in lower Glen Affric, and attempts are being made, both here and elsewhere in the Highlands, not only to preserve what is left of these woods, but also to reintroduce native species in areas where they have disappeared.

Sculpted by the sea: the Stacks of Duncansby

The pine forests are home to rare birds like the capercaillie, black grouse, crossbill and crested tit, and to mammals such as the red squirrel, pine marten, and wildcat. The lochs and rivers are rich in salmon and trout, which provide food for small populations of otter and osprey, and nesting sites for waterfowl like the red-throated diver and its rarer cousin, the black-throated diver.

In spring and early summer, huge flocks of seabirds make their nests on the sea-cliffs that fringe the coasts of Caithness, Sutherland and Easter Ross. Here the bird-watcher can see kittiwakes, fulmars, guillemots, razorbills, puffins, skuas, cormorants and great black-backed gull, while the sandy shores around Dornoch and Brora support nesting colonies of arctic tern and the rarer little tern, as well as common shore birds such as oystercatcher and ringed plover.

A few words of caution
Some of the walks described in this book are on high mountains and/or in remote areas where the consequences of getting lost, suffering an accident, or being caught out by bad weather could be serious. Don't attempt these routes (walks 23, 24, 25, 26, 27 and 28) unless you are a fit, experienced walker with full hill-walking equipment, including good boots, warm clothing, waterproofs, map and compass, spare food and drink, first aid kit, bivvy bag, torch and whistle. Always check the weather forecast before setting out, and inform someone of your intended route and the time you expect to return.

At lower levels, on still summer evenings, midges can be an unbearable nuisance, so remember to carry some insect repellent. The state of the tide can be a factor on coastal walks (though not to the extent of cutting you off if you stick to the described route), as a low or falling tide increases the likelihood of observing wildlife such as shore-feeding birds and seals hauled out on half-tide sandbanks, and provides the opportunity to explore caves and rock pools. Tide times can be obtained from newspapers and tourist information offices.

There is a long-standing tradition in Scotland of the freedom to roam in wild places, but with that freedom comes responsibility. Walkers should be aware that there are restrictions on access to certain walks during the deer-stalking season. These routes – walks 23, 24, 25 and 27 – are noted in the text, along with telephone numbers to call for access information (local tourist information offices can also advise on stalking restrictions). The stalking season officially lasts from 1st July to 15th February, but most of the activity takes place between mid-August and mid-October when the red deer stags are in prime condition. Note that it is *your* responsibility to check that no shooting is taking place before you set off; just because there is no warning sign at the start of the route does not mean that there is no stalking in progress.

During the lambing season (April and May), walkers with dogs will not be welcome on any route that passes through sheep-grazing land, and during the rest of the year dogs should always be kept under strict control in such areas. Routes which may be affected during the lambing season include walks 1, 9, 10, 19, 24 and 25.

The few walks in this guide that are not on Forestry Commission land, nature reserves, rights of way or long-established hill-walking routes are on property belonging to walker-friendly landowners. But remember that land can change hands, and that farmers and estate owners who have previously welcomed walkers can have their minds changed by the irresponsible few who leave gates open, drop litter, damage walls and fences, and allow their dogs to worry livestock. For these reasons, please obey any signs and comply with the requests of a landowner if you are asked to leave or to alter your route.

The haunting ruins of Castle Girnigoe on Noss Head

The Stacks of Duncansby

Start	Duncansby Head car park, 2 miles (3.2km) east of John o' Groats
Distance	2 miles (3.2 km)
Approximate time	1 hour
Parking	Duncansby Head car park
Refreshments	None
Ordnance Survey maps	Landranger 12 (Thurso, Wick & surrounding area), Pathfinder 41, ND37/47 (John o' Groats)

Although John o' Groats has gained fame as the most northerly point on mainland Britain (even though it isn't – that distinction belongs to nearby Dunnet Head), visitors may find the place itself, with its car park, hotel and souvenir shops, something of an anti-climax. Rather more impressive is the cliff-bound promontory of Duncansby Head, only a couple of miles to the east, where this short but spectacular walk offers wild coastal scenery, excellent bird-watching, and superb views across the Pentland Firth to the Orkney Islands.

Duncansby Head marks the entrance to the Pentland Firth, the most perilous stretch of water on the British coast. Here the tides flow between Orkney and the mainland at rates of up to 10 knots, causing whirlpools, eddies and dangerous tidal races known as the Merry Men o' Mey, the Swelkie, and the Boars of Duncansby. In strong winds, when millions of tons of moving water collide with a big ocean swell, the violence of the sea has to be seen to be believed – the windows of Duncansby Head lighthouse (220ft/67m above sea-level) have been broken by stones flung by the force of the waves.

Duncansby Head car park lies directly beneath the lighthouse (built in 1924), and on a clear day it offers a magnificent view across the Pentland Firth to the Orkney islands. The island of Stroma lies in the left foreground, and far out to sea on the right the lonely white finger of a lighthouse marks the tide-ravaged reefs of the Pentland Skerries; across the firth lie the southern islands of the Orkney archipelago: Hoy, South Walls, Flotta, Swona and South Ronaldsay; and peeking above the cliffs on the western edge of Hoy, 22 miles (35km) distant, you can just make out the square-cut summit of Britain's tallest sea-stack, the Old Man of Hoy.

A signpost opposite the car park, 'Path to Stacks of Duncansby', marks the beginning of this popular walk. The path tops a slight rise beside the triangulation pillar then descends towards the Geo of Sclaites Ⓐ. This spectacular rift is 165ft (50m) deep, and the narrow ledges in the flagstone cliffs are crowded in spring and summer with nesting seabirds. Duncansby Head is also a bird migration watch-point, where flocks of wintering geese and waders make their landfall in September and October.

The rest of the route is obvious, the path following the fence along the top of the cliffs, with grand views ahead of the Stacks of Duncansby and the natural arch of Thirle Door. A gate in the fence at the top of a grassy gully (where the path rejoins the cliff-top after leaving the Geo of Sclaites) gives access to the shore below, and at low water it is possible to scramble through the arch of Thirle Door (but check tide times carefully before attempting this). The gully has been eroded along a geological fault that separates the Caithness flagstones of Duncansby Head from the coarser and more thickly-bedded sandstones from which the stacks have been carved.

As you approach the fence at ⓑ you are rewarded with a fine view of all three stacks – the Muckle Stack (largest and furthest away), the Peedie Stack ('peedie' means 'little' in the local dialect), and the tiny Tom Thumb Stack, closest to the shore, with a fine example of a wave-cut platform visible at low tide. To get a closer look at the Muckle Stack, carefully cross the fence at ⓒ and continue on the path around to the next headland. As you pass the Peedie Stack you will see that it is not the solid, pyramidal mass that it appeared to be from the north, but a thin, delicate wafer of rock that seems almost to be on the point of collapse.

In contrast, the Muckle Stack is a substantial monolith over 200ft (61m) in height, surrounded in spring and summer by a swirling maelstrom of seabirds, including guillemots, fulmars, razorbills, puffins and arctic skuas. Looking back towards the lighthouse you can see the smaller stacks of Gibo's Craig and The Knee near the Geo of

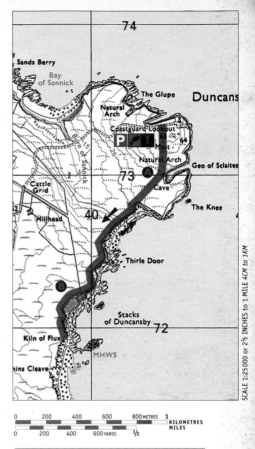

SCALE 1:25000 or 2½ INCHES to 1 MILE 4CM to 1KM

Sclaites, and beneath them the standing waves of the small tidal race called the Rispie. From the Kiln of Flux, retrace your steps back to the car park.

To see the Pentland Firth at its most turbulent, time your visit to coincide with the spectacle of the Boars of Duncansby tidal race, which is at its most impressive for a period of three hours or so, beginning about five hours after high tide at Aberdeen. As the tidal current begins to flow from west to east through the firth, a crescent of turbulent white water appears between Duncansby Head and the Pentland Skerries, and if the wind is blowing strongly in the opposite direction, the sea is whipped into a frenzy of foam and breaking waves. (The time of high tide at Aberdeen can be found in most Scottish newspapers.) ●

Craig Phadrig

Start	Leachkin Brae, Inverness
Distance	2 miles (3.2 km)
Approximate time	1 hour
Parking	Craig Phadrig car park. From central Inverness, follow signs for the A82 to Fort William, but take the first road on the right after crossing the Caledonian Canal at Tomnahuirich Bridge (signposted Muirtown). A mile (1.6km) later, turn left on Leachkin Road (signposted Craig Dunain and Craig Phadrig Hospitals), go straight across a mini-roundabout and take the first road on the right, Leachkin Brae. The car park is 150 yds (137m) along on the right
Refreshments	Pubs, restaurants and cafés in Inverness
Ordnance Survey maps	Landranger 26 (Inverness & Strathglass area), Pathfinder 177, NH 64/74 (Inverness & Culloden Muir)

The wooded hill of Craig Phadrig (564ft/172m), rising to the west of Inverness, is topped by the remains of an Iron Age fort, which may have been the stronghold of Brude, the Pictish king who was converted by St Columba in the late 6th century. Forest Enterprise has laid out a couple of waymarked paths here, including an all-abilities trail suitable for wheelchair-users, and the hill is popular with local walkers. This interesting route combines a short climb to the summit of the hill with a walk through the woods.

The walk begins at a gate at the back of the car park. Follow the blue waymarks up the hill, keeping to the right at the first three junctions, after which the path begins to climb more steeply among Scots pines and rocky outcrops towards the summit **Ⓐ** (you will notice that the rock outcrops consist of the ubiquitous Old Red Sandstone conglomerate that forms many of the hills described in this book).

The ramparts of the Iron Age fort on the summit are oval in outline, enclosing a scrub-filled depression about 260ft (79m) long and 90ft (27m)

wide; the walls were originally of stonework laced with timber, which was set on fire at some point, possibly during an attack on the fort, when the intense heat baked and partly melted the stone, fusing it together in a process called 'vitrification'. There are several such 'vitrified forts' scattered across northern Scotland, including Ord Hill (just north of the Kessock Bridge), Knock Farril (see Walk 11), and Dun Creich (across the Kyle of Sutherland from Struie Hill, Walk 15).

Excavations have ascertained that the Craig Phadrig fort dates from around

The Beauly Firth from Craig Phadrig

hear the high-pitched 'zee-zee-zee' call of the diminutive goldcrest, Britain's smallest bird. With patience and a pair of binoculars you might even see one – the body is yellowish-green, the head topped by a fiery orange crest edged with black – though these tiny birds live mostly in the tree tops and are hard to spot. At the next junction, $^1/_2$ mile (800m) later, ignore the waymark straight ahead and turn right ⬤. After five minutes' walking, just as the road begins to bend to the right, look out for a yellow waymark on the right; a few yards beyond it, fork left on a grassy track leading downhill to rejoin the outward route at the first junction and return to the start. ⬤

500 BC, and that it was occupied at the time of Brude and Columba in AD 565, but it seems that its fortifications were by then in serious disrepair, and the actual seat of the Pictish king may have been elsewhere. The summit is mostly ringed by trees, and the best views are to be had from the south-west end, where there is a fine prospect over the Beauly Firth towards Ben Wyvis and the Strathconon hills.

Follow the narrow path around the top of the earthworks (in either direction) to the far end of the fort, and descend through the forest on the north side of the hill until you meet an obvious path running horizontally across the slope. Follow this path to the left to reach a forestry track, and turn left again to a viewpoint and picnic table (yellow waymark and sign saying 'End of all-abilities trail') ⬤. The view is to the north-east, over the Kessock Bridge and the Moray Firth towards Chanonry Point and Fort George.

Return to the forestry track and turn left, following it downhill until it meets another road ⬤, then turn left again. The forest here is dark and dense, but if you stop for a few minutes you will

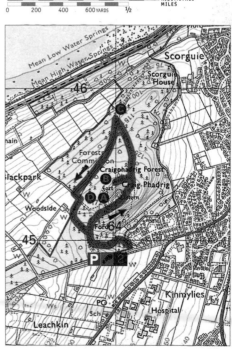

River Oich

Start	River Oich car park, 1 mile (1.6km) west of Fort Augustus on minor road to Auchteraw
Distance	4 miles (6.4 km)
Approximate time	2 hours
Parking	River Oich car park
Refreshments	None
Ordnance Survey maps	Landranger 34 (Fort Augustus & Glen Albyn area), Pathfinder 238, NH20/30 (Fort Augustus & Loch Garry)

The River Oich flows for 6 miles (9.7km) between Loch Oich and Loch Ness, running alongside one of the most scenic stretches of the Caledonian Canal. This walk follows the riverbank for 2 miles (3.2km) to a delightful picnic spot before returning through the forest and provides a welcome escape from the tourist crowds of nearby Fort Augustus and Loch Ness.

The peaceful banks of the River Oich

Leave the car park by the 'River Walk' signpost. Ignore the green/yellow waymark on the right (this is the return route) and head straight on down the hill to the bank of the River Oich. Turn right and follow the path along the riverside. Woods of beech, oak, larch and Scots pine line the grassy banks, which in spring and summer are sprinkled with wild flowers, including Scottish bluebell, hawkbit, tormentil, and the small purple globes of devil's-bit scabious. On the far side of the river you can see the embankment of the Caledonian Canal, and there is often the surreal

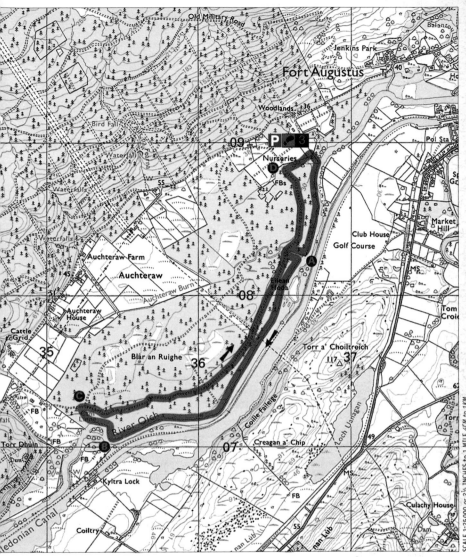

sight of yachts' masts gliding past above the bushes.

If the Auchteraw Burn Ⓐ is in spate, you may have to detour to the nearby forestry road to bridge the stream, before returning to the river by the yellow-waymarked path beyond the bridge. If the burn is dry, cut straight across the stream bed and continue along the riverbank.

After half an hour you reach a lovely picnic spot on a bend in the river Ⓑ, where a grassy sward and a little gravel beach catch the afternoon sun. Just past here the path forks twice; go left, then right, away from the river (at both forks follow the yellow waymarks), to reach a gravelled forestry road Ⓒ. Turn right and follow this road for almost 2 miles (3.2km). When a gate comes into view ahead Ⓓ, cut right on a narrow path with a green/yellow waymark, which leads back to the car park. ⬤

Ness Islands and Tomnahuirich

Start	Whin Park, Inverness
Distance	4½ miles (7.2km)
Approximate time	2½ hours
Parking	Whin Park car park. From central Inverness, follow signs for the A82 to Fort William and turn left immediately before the Tomnahuirich swing bridge over the Caledonian Canal
Refreshments	Coffee shop at nearby Floral Hall, and pubs, cafés and restaurants in Inverness
Ordnance Survey maps	Landranger 26 (Inverness), Pathfinder 177, NH64/74 (Inverness & Culloden Muir)

The River Ness flows for 6 short miles (9.7km) from Loch Ness to the sea, passing right through the heart of the Highland capital, Inverness. The beautiful Ness Islands lie at the southern edge of the town, where a cluster of wooded islets in the river has been linked together by elegant footbridges, providing the perfect setting for a stroll on a summer evening.

Take the path leading east from the car park, with the football pitch on your left and a tree-lined stream on your right. Continue on the asphalt footpath along the left bank of the River Ness as far as the hospital, then turn right across the elegant Victorian suspension footbridge Ⓐ. The river here is broad and shallow, and the view downstream takes in the red sandstone towers of St Andrew's Cathedral (built 1868), and the bluff battlements of the castle (dating from the 1830s and now the home of the Law Courts). Upstream are the wooded Ness Islands, with local salmon anglers casting in the pools and streams below.

Return upstream on the far bank of the river (called Ladies' Walk), until the path approaches the main road, then turn right across a small stream and continue along the riverside. Cross a

suspension footbridge Ⓑ on to the first of the Ness Islands. The islands, planted with beautiful woods of mature pine, fir, beech, sycamore and holly, have provided a popular retreat for the townspeople since the 19th century, and offer a variety of appealing picnic spots. You can follow either of the paths to the far end, where a green-painted footbridge leads to the second island.

Follow the path on the left to the far end of the island, then return down the opposite side to another suspension footbridge Ⓒ, which leads back to the left bank of the river to cross your outward route. Go through the gap in the wall to the left of the bridge, then cross the street and follow the road with the football pitch on your right. The road bends right, then left, to reach a T-junction with a busy road Ⓓ.

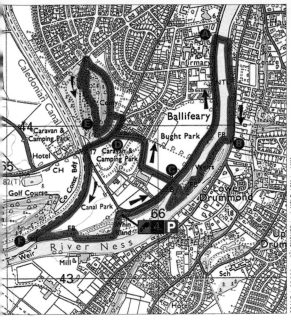

0	200	400	600	800 METRES	1
					KILOMETRES
					MILES
0	200	400	600 YARDS	½	

Statistical Account of 1793 as the 'most remarkable hill in this parish . . . a beautifully insulated mount, nearly resembling a ship with her keel uppermost. This hill in the year 1753 was enclosed and planted, chiefly with Scots firs. The elevation from the channel of the river is 250 feet.' In 1878 the hill was made into a cemetery, and it must now rank as one of the country's most beautiful burial grounds.

Descend the steep steps beyond the War Memorial. If the gate at the foot of the hill is locked, turn left to exit at the main gate. Turn right along the main road, then go left immediately before the swing bridge over the canal and head along the towpath. The canal, designed by Thomas Telford, was opened in 1822 and stretches for 60 miles (96km) from Corpach, near Fort William, to Inverness.

After ten minutes' walk, the steep bank on your left falls back to reveal a weir on the River Ness below ●. (The towpath continues for 3 miles (4.8km) to the next lock at Dochgarroch, where the canal joins Loch Dochfour, an extension of Loch Ness.) There is an old mooring bollard to the left of the towpath, and behind it a narrow path cuts back left and descends wooden steps towards the riverbank. Follow this path to the open playing fields of Canal Park and follow their right-hand edge for 200 yds (183m). Cross a footbridge signposted 'Whin Park' and take any of the paths through the park to the far end of the boating pond, where the park gate on the left, beside the ice-cream kiosk, leads back to the car park. ●

Go right for 100 yds (91m) and enter the main gate of Tomnahuirich Cemetery (open from 8am Mon–Sat, 10am Sun and local holidays; closed 4pm Nov–Feb, 5pm Mar and Oct, 6pm Apr and Sep, 7pm May–Aug; no dogs allowed). Follow the tarmac road rightwards to the far end of the burial ground, then head back left on the far side of the hill.

The road forks immediately; take the left-hand, unsurfaced branch, leading uphill. At the next junction, cut back sharp left, then follow a hairpin bend back right at a huge Celtic cross. About 50 yds (46m) after the cross, climb a flight of stairs leading up from the left side of the road, and follow the path up and right to emerge on the flat, wooded summit of the hill. Go up the steps on the right towards the War Memorial ●, where there is a fine view south over the river and the Caledonian Canal towards the Great Glen.

Tomnahuirich (Gaelic for 'hill of the yew tree') was described in the

The Black Rock of Novar

Start	Evanton
Distance	2½ miles (4km)
Approximate time	1½ hours
Parking	Car park on Evanton main street, opposite shops
Refreshments	Hotel in Evanton
Ordnance Survey maps	Landranger 21 (Dornoch, Alness & Invergordon area), Pathfinders 143, NH46/56 (Ben Wyvis) and 144, NH66/76 (Invergordon)

At first glance, the village of Evanton, founded in 1810 by local landowner Evan Fraser of Balconie, appears to have little of distinction to offer visitors. But hidden behind the town in the wooded glen of the River Glass is one of Scotland's geological wonders: the Black Rock of Novar.

From the car park, walk north along Evanton's main street, past the Novar Arms Hotel and the Black Rock caravan site. Immediately after crossing the bridge over the Allt Graad, turn left on the minor road to Glen Glass and Assynt Ⓐ. Ten minutes' walk from the main road, and about 150 yds (137m) beyond a cottage called Traum, look out for a grassy forest track leading downhill to the left Ⓑ (there is a faded orange 'Fire Danger'sign beside the road here).

Turn right at the foot of the hill and follow the occasionally muddy path upstream along the attractive, wooded banks of the Allt Graad, whose peaty brown waters flow gently among smooth,

The Allt Graad below Black Rock gorge

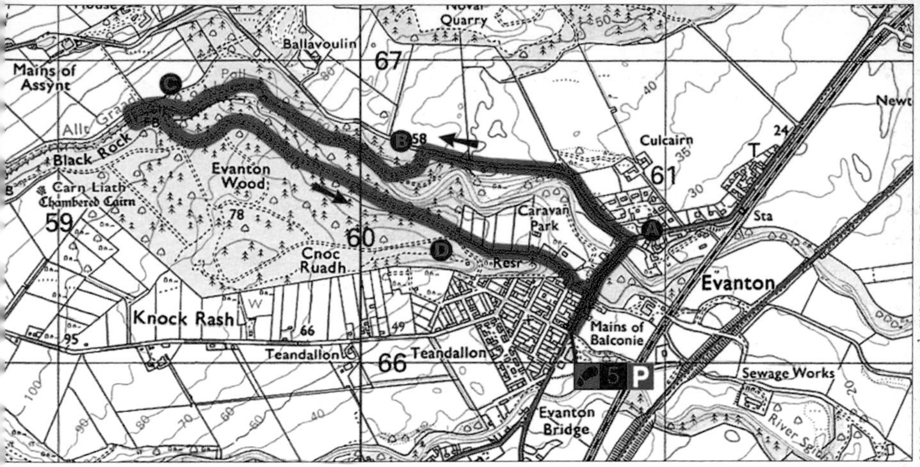
Quarry
Ballavoulin
Mains of Assynt
67
Allt Graad
Black Rock
Carn Liath Chambered Cairn
59
Evanton Wood
78
Cnoc Ruadh
60
58
Culcairn
61
Caravan Park
Resr
Sta
Evanton
Mains of Balconie
Knock Rash
Teandallon
66
Teandallon
5
P
Sewage Works
Evanton Bridge
River Sgitheach
Newt
SCALE 1:25 000 or 2½ INCHES to 1 MILE 4CM to 1KM

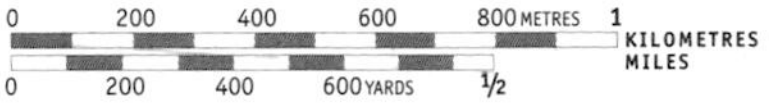
0 200 400 600 800 METRES 1 KILOMETRES
MILES
0 200 400 600 YARDS ½

rounded boulders. The river rises in Loch Glass, in the shadow of Ben Wyvis, and is known as the River Glass above the gorge, but changes its name to the Allt Graad as it enters the Black Rock gorge. In Gaelic *glas* means 'grey' and *grad* means 'sudden, quick, hasty, irascible', which neatly sums up the change in the stream's character as it enters the ravine.

Soon the path begins to climb above the river as you approach the downstream end of the gorge. At the top of the hill the path forks; keep left, then right along the wooded lip of the gorge (take great care if the path is wet, as the cliff edge is unfenced). In several places fallen tree-trunks span the top of the ravine, which grows ever narrower as you proceed upstream.

You soon arrive at a wooden footbridge **C**, from which it is possible to peer into the dark and mossy confines of the Black Rock of Novar. Named after the local Novar Estate, the Black Rock gorge is over 1 mile (1.6km) long and up to 100ft (30m) deep, but rarely more than 12ft (3.6m) wide. It was formed during the last Ice Age when glacial meltwaters from Ben Wyvis and the valley of Loch Glass, heavily laden with erosive sand and gravel, cut rapidly down through a resistant band of Old Red Sandstone conglomerate. The sinuous, overhanging walls are clad in a luxuriant growth of moss, ferns, ivy and whip-thin saplings, and the roar of the invisible stream can be heard in the misty depths far below. An Evanton man, Donald Macdonald, once jumped across the gorge (not recommended!), and it has been traversed at stream level by teams of intrepid (and well-equipped) gorge-walkers.

Cross the bridge and turn right, continuing upstream to a second footbridge, about 100 yds (91m) further on, which sits above a roaring waterfall. Cross the second bridge and turn right along a broad path, then turn right again opposite a farm gate and recross the first footbridge. This time turn left, follow the footpath uphill to a forestry road, and turn left through pleasant open woodland of larch, spruce, beech and birch for ½ mile (800m) to a crossroads in a wide clearing **D**.

Bear left along an unsurfaced road with woods on the right and fields to the left. After passing through a kissing-gate, keep right to reach a tarmac road, then immediately turn left down a narrow lane. At the main street, turn right to return to the car park. ●

Findhorn Gorge

Start	Sluie Walk car park on A940, 5 miles (8km) south of Forres
Distance	2½ miles (4km)
Approximate time	1½ hours
Parking	Sluie Walk car park
Refreshments	None
Ordnance Survey maps	Landranger 27 (Nairn & Forres), Pathfinder 162, NJ05/15 (Forres & Dallas)

The Findhorn is one of Scotland's most scenic rivers, rising deep in the heart of the Monadhliath Mountains between Kingussie and Loch Ness, and foaming through a succession of remote valleys and wooded defiles to reach the sea at Findhorn Bay (see Walk 17). The gorge at Sluie has been a tourist attraction since Victorian times, and this walk follows a traditional route along a well-made path on the eastern side of the river.

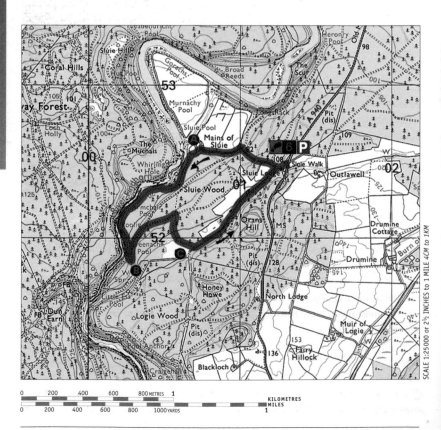

SCALE 1:25000 or 2½ INCHES to 1 MILE 4CM to 1KM

Sluie Wood is part of the Moray Estates, and the walk is waymarked throughout its length. Start along the path behind the notice-board in the car park, then turn right and continue downhill on a farm road towards the abandoned farm buildings at Mains of Sluie Ⓐ. This was once a salmon-fishing station, and Sluie Pool used to yield a rich harvest of fish, but gone are the days of the 17th century when the Earl of Moray could boast that his fishermen had caught 'at one draught, six and twenty scores' of fish – that is, 520 salmon in a single haul of the net.

Pass to the left of the buildings and follow a delightful path along the edge of the Findhorn Gorge. Mixed woodland of beech and oak, larch, fir and Scots pine borders the crags, which tower above foaming rapids and peaty brown pools. The path clings to the lip of the ravine, where the forest floor is carpeted with heather and moss, and dotted with primrose, wood anemone and forget-me-not; on the far side is the great forest of Darnaway, planted by Francis, Earl of Moray at the beginning of the 19th century. The gorge becomes deeper and more precipitous as you go further upstream, and the bedrock changes from reddish-brown sandstone to more resistant schists and gneisses.

After ½ mile (800m) you come to a wooden barrier, where a sign directs walkers to cut back left up the hillside Ⓑ. The path soon widens to a forestry road. Fork right at a junction, and right

Findhorn Gorge at Sluie

again at the next, to reach the edge of a clearing with an abandoned cottage in the middle Ⓒ. The route now bends round to the left, and follows a farm track past a few more ruined cottages to rejoin the outward route just below the car park.

There is another spectacular section of gorge 3 miles (4.8km) further south (fork right at Logie on the B9007) at Randolph's Leap, a short distance upstream from where the River Divie joins the Findhorn. Steps lead down from the road to a narrow rocky defile, at one point only 10ft (3m) across. A stone marks the height reached by the water during the catastrophic Moray floods of August 1829 – an astonishing 50ft (15m) above normal level. ●

Carbisdale Wood

Start	Culrain
Distance	2½ miles (4km)
Approximate time	2 hours
Parking	Forest Enterprise car park inside gateway to Carbisdale Castle grounds
Refreshments	Tearoom in Culrain
Ordnance Survey maps	Landranger 21 (Dornoch, Alness & Invergordon area), Pathfinder 113, NH49/59 (Strathcarron & Invershin)

A considerable amount of historic interest is packed into this short walk. The narrow, tidal waterway of the Kyle of Sutherland marks the ancient boundary between the Sutherland estates and the lands of Ross and it was here that a vengeful widow built Carbisdale Castle as a symbol of her spite against the family that spurned her. The castle is now one of the world's most opulent youth hostels.

Carbisdale Castle was built in 1906–14 for Mary Blair, the Dowager Duchess of Sutherland. She was the 3rd Duke's second wife, and when he died she

inherited his entire estate, much to the chagrin of her step-son, the 4th Duke, who contested the will. During the acrimonious court case that ensued, the duchess (who had destroyed certain documents) was found guilty of contempt of court, and served 40 days

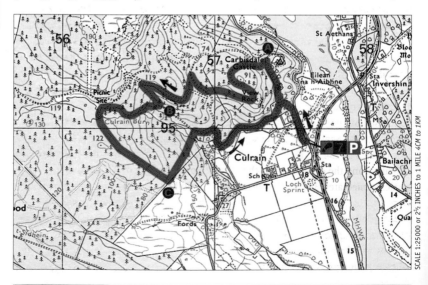

SCALE 1:25000 or 2½ INCHES to 1 MILE 4CM to 1KM

The Culrain Burn in Carbisdale Wood

eventually arrives at a junction beside a stream ⓑ. Turn right here, on the route signposted 'Picnic Site and Loch, Battle Viewpoint' and follow the blue waymarks upstream along the banks of the rocky Culrain Burn. This leads to a pretty little loch where dragonflies dart along the shore and feeding trout dimple the surface of the water around a rhododendron-covered island.

From the picnic site beside the loch, cross the dam and the footbridge beyond, then continue along a fire-break carpeted in bell heather, ling and cross-leaved heath to reach a viewpoint and information board ⓒ overlooking the site of the Battle of Carbisdale. It was here, in April 1650, that the Marquis of Montrose, fighting in the name of the deposed Charles II, clashed with government troops. Montrose had arrived in Orkney a few weeks previously with the intention of raising the country in support of the exiled king, and had occupied Thurso and Dunbeath Castle on his march south. However, his army of mercenaries was routed at Carbisdale, and Montrose fled to the west disguised as a peasant, but was soon captured and taken to Edinburgh where he was executed. The vantage point overlooking the battlefield enjoys an attractive view along the Kyle of Sutherland.

Follow the blue-waymarked path left from the viewpoint, and cross the Culrain Burn before joining a forestry road. Turn right and follow the blue/green waymarks back to the castle drive, turning right to the car park. ●

in Holloway Prison. After the settlement, in favour of the duke, the duchess married again and built Carbisdale Castle as a rival to Sutherland's seat at Dunrobin, siting it prominently above the railway, just outside the Sutherland estates, so that her hated step-son would see it every time he passed by in his private train. Her spite even extended to building a clock tower that had a clock-face on each side except the one facing east towards Sutherland, so that the duke's tenants would not benefit by it. The extraordinary castle was later purchased by the Salvesen family, who gifted it to the Scottish Youth Hostels Association in 1943.

Walk along the drive towards the castle. Immediately before the entrance to the castle precinct ⓐ, turn left on a path signposted 'Battle Site Walk, 2.5 miles'. The path, carpeted in pine needles, winds through the forest, following blue/green waymarks, and

Rogie Falls and the View Rock

Start	Rogie Falls, on the A835 just over 1 mile (1.6km) north of Contin
Distance	5 miles (8km)
Approximate time	3 hours
Parking	Rogie Falls car park
Refreshments	None
Ordnance Survey maps	Landranger 26 (Inverness & Strathglass area), Pathfinder 159, NH45/55 (Dingwall & Strathpeffer)

The View Rock above Contin has been a popular destination for walkers since Victorian times, when visitors to the spa at Strathpeffer would climb to its summit to enjoy the extensive views over the hills and glens of Easter Ross. This walk approaches the rock from the other side using Forest Enterprise trails, and starts with a visit to the spectacular Rogie Falls on the Black Water river.

From the car park, take the green-waymarked trail opposite the main road, and where the path forks, go right. This leads downhill to a junction with

Rogie Falls

another path, where you go left past a red/green/blue waymark and make a short climb to a rocky outcrop overlooking the Rogie Falls Ⓐ. Here the Black Water tumbles over two rocky steps before dropping in a single leap of 25ft (8m) into a deep, churning pool. In summer, you can watch salmon launching themselves up the falls, though the smarter fish head for the salmon ladder on the right.

Cross the suspension bridge, and continue along the path on the far bank. Where it forks, take the main branch leading uphill to the right (the left fork leads to the top of the salmon ladder). When you reach a forestry road (blue waymark) turn right.

About ½ mile (800m) along this road you arrive at a junction with a broad turning area for forestry vehicles Ⓑ. Turn left and follow another forestry

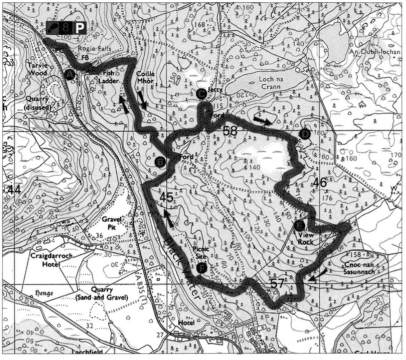

SCALE 1:25000 or 2½ INCHES to 1 MILE 4CM to 1KM

```
0      200    400    600    800 METRES  1
                                          KILOMETRES
                                          MILES
0      200    400    600 YARDS  ½
```

road uphill until you can see Loch na Crann up ahead ⓒ; look out for an old, grassy forestry road leading downhill to the right and disappearing into the trees. This soon joins a broad trail with a green waymark, where you turn left.

The trail leads across a clearing. Soon after it re-enters the trees ⓓ, turn right on a path with more green waymarks, which meanders through open forest before arriving at the summit of the View Rock ⓔ (the path forks immediately before the summit outcrop; go right here). On a good day the rock is well named, with fine views of the surrounding hills, including the distinctive conical peak of Sgurr a' Mhuilinn on the western horizon beyond little Loch Achilty, and the great bulk of Ben Wyvis rising to the north.

After admiring the view, head downhill through mixed woodland of beech, birch, pine and fir, following the green-waymarked path to the east of the summit. At the foot of the hill, the path goes through a gate and continues through a birch wood to reach a gravelled road. Cross the road and follow the path (now blue/green waymarks) across two more forestry roads to reach the picnic site and car park near Contin ⓕ.

Bear right through the car park and follow the red-waymarked track leading north along the riverbank. At the second red waymark keep straight on along a forest path. Soon after crossing a small stream on some wooden planks, an anglers' path drops down towards the riverbank, but the route keeps straight ahead and climbs high above the river, before bending to the right and following the bank of a tributary burn to reach the main forestry road near the junction at ⓑ. Turn left to retrace the initial part of the walk and return to the car park. ●

Brora to Carn Liath Broch

Start	Brora
Distance	8½ miles (13.7km)
Approximate time	4 hours
Parking	Back Shore car park in Brora. From the bridge in the centre of town, take the street along the south side of the river and follow signs to Back Shore and Beach
Refreshments	Pubs and tearooms in Brora
Ordnance Survey maps	Landranger 17 (Helmsdale & Strath of Kildonan), Pathfinder 106, NC80/90 (Brora)

The straggling seaside town of Brora once earned a living from coal-mining, salt panning, fish-curing and brick-making, but now depends largely on tourism, a small industrial estate and the Clynelish distillery. There are several good walks in the area – north along the fine, sandy beach; west by the river to lovely Loch Brora; and this one, south along the shore to the fascinating broch of Carn Liath.

Walk along the road beyond the car park towards the fenced compound of the old radio station, then bear left along a grassy path between the compound and the sea. This is the start of a coastal footpath which leads along the shore for 6 miles (9.7km), all the way to Golspie.

The path passes the old golf course, with views across the Moray Firth to the Grampian hills and the finger of Tarbat Ness with its prominent white lighthouse tower. Ahead you can see the Sutherland Monument atop Ben Bhraggie (see Walk 18), and to its left the dark bulk of Ben Wyvis. To the right of the path, an overgrown earthen mound and brick wall with rusting iron frames and pulley wheels is the former Territorial Army rifle range.

Beyond the little waterfall of the Sputie Burn Ⓐ, the cliffs rise in outcrops of soft, grey and golden-brown Jurassic sandstone, haunted by fulmars and great black-backed gulls. The foreshore is patrolled by squads of oystercatchers and ringed plovers, and you will also see black-headed gulls, curlews, and wheatears, and noisy gangs of rooks and hoodie crows scavenging along the strand line. The

The Iron Age fortification of Carn Liath Broch

Caithness, Sutherland, Skye, Orkney and Shetland. They are thought to have been built in the 1st century BC and the 1st century AD.

To enter the broch, go up the track on its west side, where there is a gate giving access to the fenced enclosure. The structure is very similar in plan to the famous broch of Dun Telve at Glenelg, on the west coast, though it is not as well preserved. Circular, drystone walls stand to a height of about 6ft (2m), and enclose an area about 30ft (9m) in diameter. The entrance passage still has its lintel, door-checks and bar-hole, and a guard cell on the right-hand side is intact. The walls are about 12ft (3.6m) thick, and on the left a section of the staircase survives within the walls. Return to Brora by the same route. ●

rocks just offshore are a favourite haul-out point for the local common seals.

About 1½–2 hours of easy walking will bring you to the broch of Carn Liath ●. Brochs are distinctive Iron Age fortifications that occur throughout Scotland, but are concentrated in

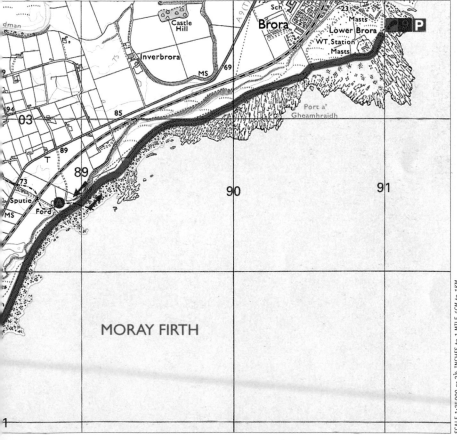

SCALE 1:25 000 or 2½ INCHES to 1 MILE 4CM to 1KM

Noss Head

Start	Staxigoe, 2 miles (3.2km) north-east of Wick
Distance	5½ miles (8.9km)
Approximate time	2½ hours
Parking	Staxigoe harbour
Refreshments	None
Ordnance Survey maps	Landranger 12 (Thurso,Wick & surrounding area), Pathfinder 58, ND25/35 (Wick)

The coastline to the north of Wick is typical of Caithness, with flagstone cliffs riven by rocky inlets (known as 'geos'). This walk follows the cliff-tops from Staxigoe to Noss Head, where the atmospheric ruins of Castle Girnigoe perch precariously on a sea-girt crag. The route passes through fields which may contain sheep and cattle and therefore dogs should not be taken on it.

The little harbour of Staxigoe was once a centre for the export of grain from Caithness to the ports of Leith, Newcastle, Hamburg and Bergen, and the granaries built there by the Earl of Caithness in the 18th century still overlook the cove. By 1800 herring fishing had taken over as the main source of income, and activity was focused on Staxigoe until the development of Wick harbour in the early 1800s. Staxigoe's quay of distinctive vertically-laid masonry was built in 1830, and at the height of the herring fishery there were 31 boats working out of the harbour. Today it is home to a handful of local lobster boats, and is also used as a launching point by visiting scuba divers.

From the harbour, head north along the private road to Field of Noss farm (sign saying 'Walkers Welcome'). Bear right through the farmyard and go through the gate into a field (remember to leave all gates as you found them). Follow the fence along the top of the cliffs (a stile gives access to the foreshore, where there are extensive outcrops of flagstone) and pass through a second gate. At the end of the next field **Ⓐ**, carefully cross the fence on your right at the strongpost, and continue along a narrow path that follows closely the top of the sea-cliffs. There are fine views ahead of the rock-bound coast, while the springy turf along the cliff-tops offers a choice of picnic spots.

At the north side of the rocky inlet called the Scholl **Ⓑ**, cross the stile and head for the obvious gate in the stone wall ahead. Cross the old iron gate, and bear left across the field, following a faint path alongside a line of old iron fence posts. At the road, turn right to take a look at the Noss Head lighthouse, built in 1849 by Alan Stevenson (an uncle of Robert Louis Stevenson). The keepers' cottages are in the so-called Egyptian style, and across the flagstone-paved courtyard lie a stable and gighouse. Return along the road to the car park just outside the gate to the lighthouse steading **Ⓒ**.

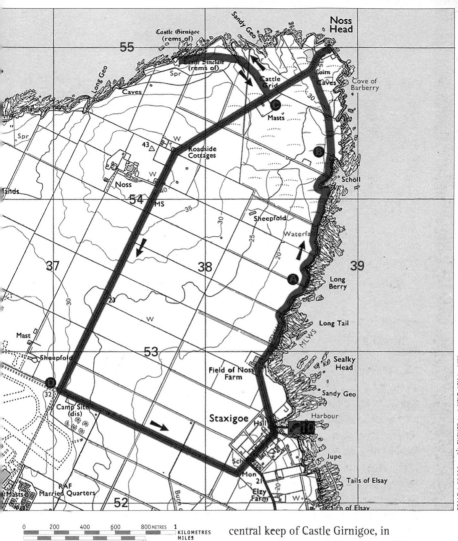

SCALE 1:25000 or 2½ INCHES to 1 MILE 4CM to 1KM

Cross the stile opposite the car park and follow the broad, well-worn path down to the sea-cliffs to visit the ruins of castles Sinclair and Girnigoe. Castle Girnigoe was built in the late 15th century by William Sinclair, 2nd Earl of Caithness, on a spectacularly narrow finger of land jutting above the sea. Castle Sinclair, an impressive Renaissance-style edifice, was added in 1607 at the landward end of the older fortress, but both were badly damaged by artillery during a siege in 1690. The most prominent remnant is the great central keep of Castle Girnigoe, in whose dungeon the 4th Earl starved his son to death; a locked gate prevents access, as the building is in a dangerous condition. A single chimney stack is all that remains of Castle Sinclair.

Return to the car park and turn right along the minor road that heads back towards Staxigoe and Wick. At the crossroads ⬤ (a sign says 'Road ahead closed') go left. The road ahead once crossed the runway at Wick Airport, which was originally a base for the RAF's Coastal Command in World War II. When you reach the school at the edge of Staxigoe village, keep straight ahead to return to the harbour. ●

Knock Farril and Cnoc Mor

Start	Strathpeffer
Distance	4½ miles (7.2km); shorter version 3½ miles (5.6km)
Approximate time	2½ hours (1½ hours for shorter walk)
Parking	Blackmuir Wood car park. Turn off main road at youth hostel at south end of town
Refreshments	Hotels and tearooms in Strathpeffer
Ordnance Survey maps	Landranger 26 (Inverness & Strathglass area), Pathfinder 159 NH45/55 (Dingwall & Strathpeffer)

Strathpeffer was once a fashionable spa resort which advertised itself as the 'Harrogate of the North', where Victorian tourists would come to take the sulphurous spring waters and relax in the comfort of the many luxury hotels. Walking was considered a healthy diversion, and the nearby summits of View Rock, Ord Hill, Cnoc Mor and Knock Farril were all popular destinations. The full walk, which includes sections that can be slippery, visits the latter two hills, partly following the route of a Victorian carriage drive; the shorter version omits the visit to Cnoc Mor.

Walk back towards the car park entrance, and take the path on the left with the red/blue/green waymark post. The path meanders pleasantly through Blackmuir Wood (follow the blue/green waymarks) before emerging from the trees at the Touchstone Maze Ⓐ. The wood contains larch, spruce, birch, rowan and bird cherry, and its mossy floor supports a rich crop of fungi, including the little golden trumpets of chanterelles and the distinctive red and white caps of fly agaric. The maze – a local arts project – includes specimens of rock from all over Scotland.

Take the path that leads away from the far side of the maze, and turn left along a forestry road which soon merges with another road coming in from the right (bear left here). The road, which was laid out as a carriage drive in the year of Queen Victoria's Jubilee,

passes through a gate and continues along the north slope of a steep-sided ridge, with grand views across Strathpeffer to Ben Wyvis. The steep slopes above are clad in bracken, moss and heather, and in summer the grassy verge is liberally sprinkled with the tiny yellow blossoms of tormentil and the lilac spikes of bugle.

The track climbs gently to a broad saddle Ⓑ below the Iron Age vitrified fort of Knock Farril. Climb the broad grassy ridge to the summit and inspect the tumbled stone of the fortifications, where you will find dark, glassy trickles of molten rock, evidence that the walls were subjected to the fierce heat of some ancient conflagration. Archaeologists once thought that such forts were fired deliberately to strengthen the walls, but today the consensus of opinion is that the fires were either accidental or the result of an enemy attack. The name Knock Farril probably derives from the Gaelic for 'hill of watching', and the fort's strategic importance is obvious from the magnificent views it commands over the approach from the Cromarty Firth at Dingwall.

The ridge of Knock Farril is composed of a hard band of Old Red Sandstone conglomerate, while the valley of Strathpeffer to the north is underlain by softer siltstones and mudstones. Interbedded with these rocks are layers of so-called 'fetid shales' which contain decayed organic matter, and it is these that give rise to the sulphurous spring waters that made Strathpeffer a popular Victorian spa.

After exploring the fort, return to the saddle at **B** and keep straight on along

an obvious path that winds through a patch of gorse before climbing on to the crest of the ridge ahead. The path follows the ridge, which is known locally as the Cat's Back, with lovely views left over Loch Ussie to the Black Isle and right to Ben Wyvis and the Strathconon hills, with the houses of Strathpeffer nestling in the valley below. At the edge of the woods the path passes through a kissing-gate **C** to meet a forestry road.

The walk can be shortened at this point by turning right, and then left at the next junction, to follow the main forestry road back to the car park.

To continue on the full route to Cnoc Mor, turn left, then right, and follow the

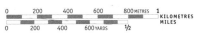

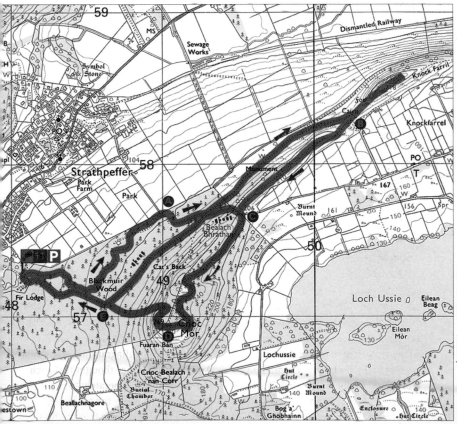

forestry road as it passes through a dark plantation and then contours around the hillside. As it passes around the second shoulder, a side road cuts steeply uphill to the right; follow this up to the triangulation pillar at the summit of Cnoc Mor ⓓ (882ft/269m).

Go across the stile behind the triangulation pillar, and follow a narrow path through the pines as it descends slightly then contours round to the right into the narrow, tree-filled notch immediately to the north of Cnoc Mor summit. When you have completed a near semi-circle, and can see a fence with a stile ahead, cut back left towards Strathpeffer on a narrow path that descends steeply in a straight line down the forested hillside (take care – this path can be very slippery, especially after rain).

The path emerges on a forestry road, with a blue/green waymark on the right ⓔ. Turn left and follow the road to Fir Lodge, where a right turn down the hill leads back to the car park.   ●

The spa town of Strathpeffer from Knock Farril

Chanonry Point
and the Fairy Glen

Start	Rosemarkie
Distance	7 miles (11.3km) Shorter version 4½ miles (7.2km)
Approximate time	3½ hours (2 hours for shorter walk)
Parking	Rosemarkie, north end of promenade
Refreshments	Hotels and tearoom in Rosemarkie and Fortrose
Ordnance Survey maps	Landranger 27 (Nairn & Forres), Pathfinder 160, NH65/75 (Fortrose & Munlochy)

This varied walk divides neatly into two parts, each of which can be done separately if desired. The first half follows the coast around the shingle spit of Chanonry Point, a popular dolphin-spotting area, while the second half climbs the hills behind Fortrose to obtain a panoramic view of the inner Moray Firth, before descending via the scenic waterfalls of the Fairy Glen.

Walk south along the promenade and where the road turns away from the sea, bear left along the grassy path between the caravan park and the shore. At the golf club car park, keep left again, on a sandy path through the coarse grass between the golf course and the shore (sign 'Pedestrians only'). In spring the grass above the beach is rich in wild flowers, including harebell (Scottish bluebell), yellow rattle, eyebright, and meadow saxifrage.

Continue to the gravel spit beyond the lighthouse Ⓐ. The promontories of Chanonry Point and Fort George are the remains of a terminal moraine – a huge ridge of boulder clay, sand and gravel – that was dumped here by a retreating tongue of ice at the end of the last Ice Age. Since then, the sea has breached the ridge and tidal currents have reworked the sand and gravel into its present form – you will notice that many of the pebbles on the beach are of

grey schist and quartzite that originated in the Highlands, many miles to the west. The tide still sluices through the narrows here at such a rate that yachts and other small boats must wait for a fair tide in order to pass through.

The point is a favourite spot for dolphin watchers, who gather here to catch a glimpse of the Moray Firth's famous colony of bottle-nose dolphins (the most northerly in Europe). It is also a good place to watch porpoises, seals and seabirds. Walk along the beach on the far side of the lighthouse to the car park beyond the jetty. (At high tide you may have to retrace your steps for 100 yds (91m) and use the road Ⓑ that cuts across on the landward side of the lighthouse.) Continue on a path beside the shore, past a cottage and a half-buried 19th-century ice-house to the 6th tee of the golf course (another sign saying 'Pedestrians only'). Continue along the beach or the faint path along the edge of the golf course (the red poles mark the boundary of the course).

At the far end of the golf course, follow the tarmac road through the caravan site, but where the road bends away from the shore, bear left along a broad grassy path above the sea. The path emerges at a picnic site. From there, follow the tarmac road into Fortrose, passing Fortrose Academy on the right and St Andrew's Church on the left before turning right into Cathedral Square. Go left around the square to

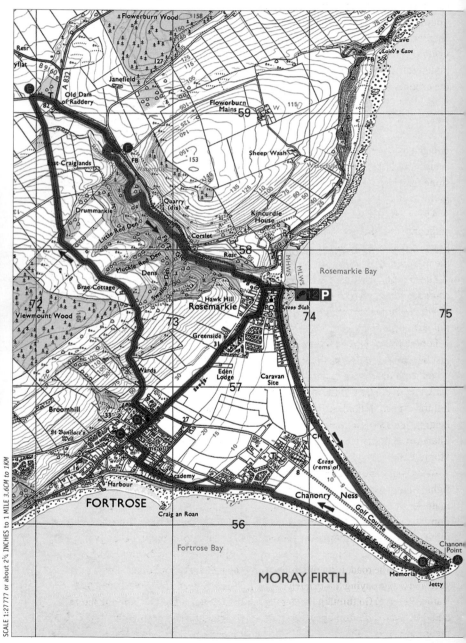

SCALE 1:27777 or about 2¼ INCHES to 1 MILE 3.6CM to 1KM

reach the entrance to the cathedral precinct 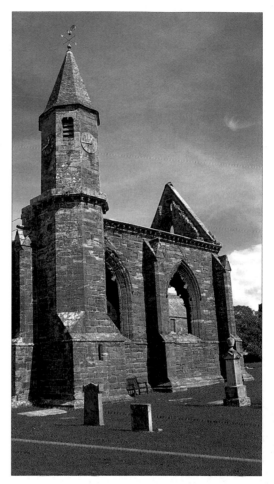.

Fortrose Cathedral was once a splendid Gothic church, dating from the 13th–15th centuries, but all that remains standing is the south aisle, containing the canopied tomb of Euphemia, Countess of Ross, and the chapter house, with a vaulted 13th-century undercroft; the outline of the original building is marked on the ground. It was sacked during the Reformation, and then pillaged by Cromwell's troops to provide building stone for a fort at Inverness in the 1650s.

After visiting the cathedral, turn right past the Royal Hotel and head along the main street.

For the shorter walk, continue along this road for ³⁄₄ mile (1.2km) to return to the start.

For the full walk, turn left just beyond the pink sandstone church on a minor road signposted 'Hill walk to Raddery', and follow it over the hill for 2 miles (3.2km). As you gain height, a magnificent view opens over Chanonry Point, Fort George and the Moray Firth.

At the T-junction near Raddery turn right, and then right again at the main A832 road by the telephone box. Continue downhill until you see the minor road to Eathie signposted on the left; just past this point, on the right-hand side of the road, is an old iron gate and a sign saying 'Fairy Glen Nature Reserve'. Go through the gate and descend to a footbridge below a picturesque waterfall.

The remains of Fortrose Cathedral

The route now follows a path beside the Rosemarkie Burn as it tumbles through pools and waterfalls cut into the sandstone bedrock. In spring the wooded glen is bright with bluebells, primrose, red campion and wood sorrel, and dippers and kingfishers haunt the stream. Lower down, a mill lade from the burn flows through an 18th-century 'pow' or pond, once used for the steeping of flax before it was taken to the mill at the foot of the glen.

The path emerges on to the A832 road beside a bridge. Continue along the road, and turn left at the Plough Inn to return to the starting point. ●

Farigaig Forest

Farigaig Forest

Start	Inverfarigaig, on the B852, 14 miles (22km) south of Inverness
Distance	5½ miles (8.9km) Shorter version 3 miles (4.8km)
Approximate time	3 hours (1½ hours for shorter walk)
Parking	Farigaig Forest Centre car park
Refreshments	None
Ordnance Survey maps	Landranger 26 (Inverness & Strathglass area), Pathfinder 208, NH42/52 (Mid Loch Ness)

The road along the south side of Loch Ness follows the route of General Wade's military road from Inverness to Fort Augustus, and is quieter and more scenic than the busy A82 on the far bank. Halfway down the loch is the Farigaig Forest Centre, the starting point for this walk, which enjoys some superb views over Loch Ness, and gives a magnificent display of autumn colours in September and October.

Start out on the yellow-waymarked footpath that leads uphill behind the Forest Enterprise Visitor Centre, and take the right-hand fork, signposted 'Loch Ness Viewpoint'. The path climbs up the mossy hillside through birch and pine to a rocky outcrop with a bench overlooking Loch Ness. Beyond the viewpoint, the path meanders across a ridge and then descends to a forest road. Turn right here and head uphill.

After 200 yds (183m), look out for a yellow waymark on the left, and climb the steps up to another forest road, where you turn right. Follow this road until it swings sharply round to the left ⓐ, then turn on to a narrow footpath on the right to cross a cleared area and re-enter the forest. The route now turns left and climbs steeply uphill past a bench to a ridge and a yellow waymark.

A short detour to the left leads to a fine picnic spot on a granite outcrop upholstered with heather cushions and

flanked by moss-draped birches. There is a magnificent view over Loch Ness to Urquhart Castle and Drumnadrochit Bay and, round to the left, the prominent summit of Meallfuarvonie (see Walk 20). Straight ahead, across the deep Pass of Inverfarigaig, rise the cliffs of Dùn Dearduil, capped by an Iron Age vitrified fort.

Return to the waymark and fork left downhill to rejoin the forest road near Lochan Torr an Tuill. Turn right and continue on the grassy road for ¾ mile (1.2km) until you reach a minor road ⓑ. Turn left and follow the road along a wooded glen. As the glen narrows below the crags of Creag an Fhithich, a forest track, signposted 'Footpath to Aultnagoire and Stratherrick', bridges the stream on the right ⓒ.

The walk can be shortened at this point by continuing along the road to a junction beside a bridge, and turning left ⓗ to return to Inverfarigaig.

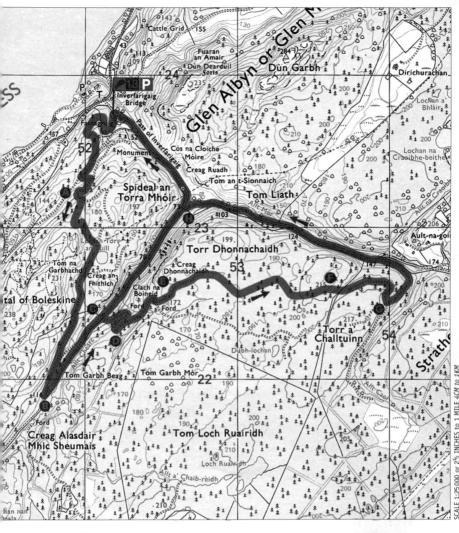

0	200	400	600	800 METRES	1		
						KILOMETRES	
						MILES	
0	200	400	600 YARDS	½			

For the full walk, follow the mossy track as it switchbacks up the densely forested hillside. The second hairpin bend **Ⓓ** is not immediately obvious – you arrive in a clearing with a birch tree in the middle and an inviting path leading straight ahead, but the route cuts back left here, along a broad mossy track that is partly concealed by the trees. Soon after crossing a small watercourse the track forks; go right. Then, as the path swings around to the right **Ⓔ**, go left through an obvious gap in the trees to reach a new, gravelled forestry road.

Turn left on the forestry road, heading in an easterly direction, and follow it to its end at a cleared area with a wooden fence and gate visible ahead **Ⓕ**. Go through the gate (the gatepost has Forest Enterprise waymark arrows), and follow the path beyond it along a fire-break with a drystone dyke on the left. The path soon broadens into a pleasant grassy track that contours around to the right before arriving at a clearing and a crossroads **Ⓖ**.

Turn left down a forestry road whose asphalt surface has long since been overgrown with grass, to emerge at a wooden gate beside the minor road between Inverfarigaig and Errogie. Turn left and follow the road down through the glen, passing the junction ● where the shorter walk rejoins the main route. This is the Pass of Inverfarigaig, a picturesque, steep-sided valley clad in native woodland of birch, beech, ash, hazel and rowan, with a burn tumbling down amid huge, moss-covered boulders. Near the foot of the glen, on the left-hand side of the road, is a granite monument to James Bryce, a distinguished Victorian geologist who fell to his death nearby in 1877. ●

Farigaig Forest

Covesea Coast

Start	Hopeman, 6 miles (9.7km) north of Elgin
Distance	8½ miles (13.7km)
Approximate time	4 hours
Parking	On east side of Hopeman harbour
Refreshments	Pub in Hopeman
Ordnance Survey maps	Landranger 28 (Elgin, Dufftown & surrounding area), Pathfinder 146, NJ16/26 (Elgin)

Hopeman is a pleasant holiday village, with good sandy beaches on either side of the picturesque harbour. It is noted for the production of Hopeman stone, an attractive golden-brown sandstone, from the nearby Greenbrae and Clashach quarries. The neighbouring coast is riddled with caves and natural arches, many linked with tales of smugglers. This walk explores the coast to the east as far as Covesea before returning inland via Gordonstoun and the village of Duffus, and a diversion (for the sure-footed only) gives access at low tide to the romantically named Sculptors' Cave.

The town of Hopeman was laid out in 1805 by William Young of Inverugie, who later gained notoriety as the Commissioner of the Duke of Sutherland's Estates – the man who oversaw the beginning of the infamous Highland Clearances (see Walk 18). The harbour was added in 1837 by Admiral Archibald Duff of Drummuir to encourage the herring fishing.

From the parking area, walk back towards the town, but turn along the first street on the left, between the beach and the football pitch. At the road end, a sandy path continues past a row of beach huts and heads along the coast below the golf course. There is a bench near the point, with good views across the Moray Firth to the hills of Sutherland and Caithness – the cone of Morven (see Walk 25) and the three-humped ridge of Scaraben are easily

picked out. Looking east along the coast you can see the cliffs of golden-brown Permian sandstone, scarred by rubble from Clashach quarry and topped by the tower of the old Coastguard Lookout.

After passing a hollow containing the 12th green of the golf course Ⓐ, bear right up the hill and along a sandy path through the gorse, overlooking a little cove with a deep cave in the far side. The path passes the 11th green then turns inland to meet a gravel road. Turn left towards the yellow gate at the entrance to Clashach Quarry, but bear right just before it on a track marked 'Coastal Path', which skirts the quarry and then cuts through the large expanse of gorse that lines the clifftop. The gorse is the haunt of stonechats, the males resplendent in their summer plumage of bright chestnut breast, glossy black head and white neck patches.

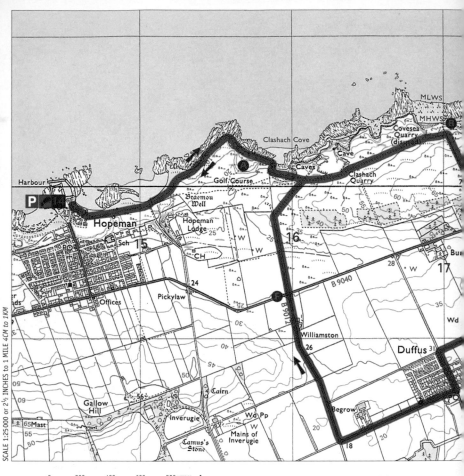

SCALE 1:25 000 or 2½ INCHES to 1 MILE 4CM to 1KM

At a small clearing with an old iron stile ⑬, the path ahead becomes overgrown with gorse, so head uphill, turning right away from the sea on a broad, easy path with an old, rusty fence on the right. When you draw level with a pair of radio masts, turn left and go around the fenced enclosure to the road on the far side, and follow it past a second mast installation. Turn left and follow the road down to the white Coastguard Lookout tower.

To the right of the lookout, wooden steps lead down towards the sea, and a narrow path continues along the clifftop. A steep ladder in a rocky cleft below the steps gives access to the foreshore, where it is possible to scramble back west for 200 yds (183m) to the so-called Sculptors' Cave, whose walls are said to bear Pictish carvings – they are certainly covered in abundant graffiti, some of them over a hundred years old. (This diversion is only for sure-footed walkers who have checked the tide times.)

The route continues past a shingle cove with a two-legged sea stack, and beneath the white houses at Covesea Village to join a broad, grassy track; take the lower fork, which slopes down past some sandstone outcrops to the sandy beach of Covesea Links, with a small golf course on the right. The name Covesea, which applies also to the nearby lighthouse and the offshore skerries, is pronounced 'causie', and is

46 ● WALK 14

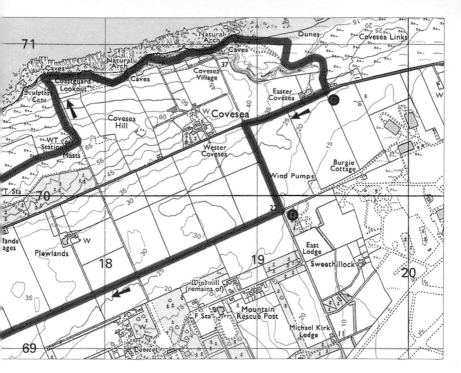

said to derive from an ancient causeway which once ran across nearby Loch Spynie (long since drained and converted to farmland). Turn right beyond the 1st green of the golf course, go through the wooden gate, and follow the sandy track on the left uphill to the B9040 road ●.

Turn right along the B9040 for 500 yds (457m), then go left along a minor road for another 500 yds (457m), and turn right ● on a farm road that runs straight for 1½ miles (2.4km) to the village of Duffus. About halfway along, a drive on the left allows a glimpse of the exclusive Gordonstoun School (not open to the public), where the Duke of Edinburgh, the Prince of Wales, the Duke of York and Prince Edward were educated. The main house, the oldest parts of which date from the early 17th century, was once the seat of the Barony of Gordonstoun; the school was founded by the German educationalist Dr Kurt Hahn in 1934.

At the T-junction in Duffus, turn left to emerge on the main road beside the village shop ●. A short detour to the left here, along the road to Gordonstoun, brings you to the ruins of St Peter's Church, with a fine porch dating from 1524 and a 14-ft (4m) high kirkyard cross. Return to the shop and keep straight on, out of the village, and follow the B9012 around to the right. Where it meets the B9040 ●, go straight across and continue along an unsurfaced road towards Clashach Quarry to rejoin the outward route just before the second yellow gate (with the 'Coastal Path' sign). Turn left to return to the start.   ●

The harbour at Hopeman

Struie Hill

Start	B9176, 2½ miles (4km) south of its junction with the A836 near Easter Fearn
Distance	4 miles (6.4 km)
Approximate time	2½ hours
Parking	Parking area on west side of B9176, ½ mile (800m) south of viewpoint on the B9176
Refreshments	None
Ordnance Survey maps	Landranger 21 (Dornoch, Alness & Invergordon area), Pathfinder 123, NH68/78 (Tain)

The B9176 climbs through the pass known as the Cadha Mor, 'the great entrance', on the old drove road between Sutherland and the rich cattle markets of the south. The herds were driven down from the northern hills, and swum across the Kyle of Sutherland at the narrows of am bonnath, 'the bottom ford', which gave its name to Bonar Bridge. The pass is dominated by the steep ridge of Struie Hill, an easy climb which rewards the walker with splendid views across the Kyle of Sutherland and the Dornoch Firth.

The Kyle of Sutherland from the viewpoint below Struie Hill

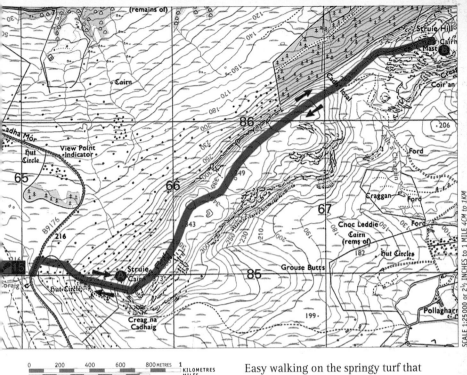

SCALE 1:25 000 or 2½ INCHES to 1 MILE 4CM to 1KM

Walk north along the main road for about 100 yds (91m), almost as far as the triangular road sign. From here, begin climbing on a well-trodden path that heads up the hillside, skirting the left end of a small stand of Scots pines. As you gain height, look left along the north-west flank of Struie Hill, and note the sudden change of slope at the foot of the crags which marks the geological fault where the wedge of resistant conglomerate that forms the summit ridge has been thrust over older and more easily eroded schists.

The path leads easily up to a cairn marking the south-western end of the long ridge of Struie Hill. Examine the outcrops of Old Red Sandstone conglomerate and note the pebbles of granite and quartzite that it contains. There is also a large boulder of granite here, a glacial erratic that was deposited by retreating ice sheets at the end of the last Ice Age.

Easy walking on the springy turf that coats the flat top of the ridge leads to the saddle at Cadh Iosal, from where a rough road takes you to the radio mast on the north-east summit ⑬. Although this end of the ridge is 130ft (40m) lower than the south-west top, its position overlooking the Dornoch Firth provides a much better viewpoint.

The panorama to the east extends over the narrows of Meikle Ferry and the modern road bridge to the spire of Dornoch Cathedral and beyond to the hills of east Sutherland and the monument to the first Duke of Sutherland on Ben Bhraggie (see Walk 18); on the south shore of the firth is the Royal Burgh of Tain, and in the distance the low promontory of Tarbat Ness. Looking west, you can see the Kyle of Sutherland and Strath Oykel snaking into the distance, the villages of Ardgay and Bonar Bridge, and perhaps a glimpse of Loch Shin; to the south lie the lonely hills of Easter Ross. From here, retrace your steps back to the starting point. ●

The Speyside Way

The Speyside Way

Start	Tugnet Icehouse, Spey Bay, 6 miles (9.7km) north of Fochabers
Distance	10 miles (16.1km)
Approximate time	4 hours
Parking	Car park at Tugnet Icehouse
Refreshments	Hotel at Spey Bay, restaurant at Baxters Visitor Centre
Ordnance Survey maps	Landranger 28 (Elgin, Dufftown & surrounding area), Pathfinders 147, NJ36/46 (Buckie) and 163, NJ25/35 (Fochabers & Glen of Rothes)

The Spey is Scotland's second-longest river (after the Tay), famed for its salmon fishing and its whisky distilleries. The river rises in lonely Loch Spey beneath the Corrieyairack Pass (see Walk 28) and flows for 98 miles (158km) to the Moray Firth at Spey Bay. This walk explores the river's last few miles before it enters the sea, following the Speyside Way long-distance footpath as far as the road bridge at Fochabers, and returning via a quiet country road and the 19th-century Spey Viaduct.

Tugnet Icehouse, at the mouth of the River Spey, was built in 1831 and is the largest building of its kind in Scotland. It was once used to store ice for the local salmon fishermen – the walls are dug into the ground and the roof covered in turf to provide insulation – but now houses a museum describing the history of the Spey salmon fishery. The shingle bar at the mouth of the river is a good place to spot seals and, occasionally, bottle-nosed dolphins. A new mouth for the river was cut here in 1989, as the old course had been threatening to wash away the village of Kingston on the far bank.

Go through the gate to the right of the information board, and follow the path along the bank of the river to join a farm road heading south along the edge of a wood. From here on, follow the Speyside Way waymarks (wooden posts with a white thistle logo). This long-distance footpath was opened in 1981, and currently runs from Spey Bay to Bridge of Avon (with a spur to Tomintoul), and there are plans to extend it south to Aviemore and east along the coast to Buckie.

The path stays away from the river for the first 1 or 2 miles (1.6–3.2km) before joining the east bank Ⓐ, which it follows up to Fochabers. Here the Spey flows its final few miles to the sea amid huge shingle banks which are regularly flooded and rearranged when the river is in spate. The worst recorded flood was in August 1829, when the river flowed a mile wide at this point.

River Spey

These lower stretches are also some of the most sought-after salmon beats on the river, and in season you will see anglers on the banks casting hopefully into the stream.

As you near the A96 road bridge, the path leaves the riverbank and follows the crest of an old embankment through Bellie Wood. Ignore the Speyside Way signs that you have been following so far, and pass beneath the bridge and the older bridge beyond it. Bear left along a wooded path, and after about 50 yds (46m) you will see a concrete marker with the letter 'H' to the left ●. Cut back left here, up the embankment to a gate, and turn left to cross the old road bridge over the Spey (now a footpath and cycle route). There is a grand view from the bridge, looking upstream along the river towards Ben Rinnes (see Walk 21) and the Hills of Cromdale.

At the far end of the road bear right past the Old Toll House and continue along the asphalt footpath opposite Baxters Factory and Visitor Centre. Baxters of Speyside was founded in 1868 by George Baxter, a former gardener for the Duke of Richmond and Gordon, and the business is still run by his descendants. The company holds Royal Warrants from the Queen and Queen Mother as Fruit Canners and Purveyors of Scottish Specialities.

Cross the main road at the traffic island as you enter the village of Mosstodloch. Turn into the first street on the right (just past the Ben Aigan pub) ●, and follow this minor road for 3 miles (4.8km) towards Garmouth. On the way you will pass Speymouth parish church, known as the 'Red Kirk', set in an attractive glebe of mature beech and sycamore trees; and Essil Old Cemetery, which contains many interesting gravestones including a couple of 18th-century table-stones. The surrounding fields are the haunt of yellowhammers, and on summer evenings the sky is filled with swallows and sand martins hawking for insects.

Garmouth claimed its place in Scottish history when King Charles II landed here on 23 June 1650 after returning from exile in Europe. Today it is a pleasantly haphazard village that comes alive on the last Saturday in June, when it celebrates the Maggie Fair, a traditional country fête. The nearby village of Kingston was named by merchants from Kingston-upon-Hull, who founded it as a port and shipbuilding centre in the 1780s. Over 300 ships were built here, many of them clippers, using timber floated down the Spey, before the industry declined in the late 19th century.

As you reach the sign marking the edge of Garmouth village ●, a flight of wooden steps to the right of the road leads down to a footpath on the line of the old railway. Follow this across the Spey Viaduct, which was built by the Great North of Scotland Railway Company in 1886 at a cost of £100,000, and at the time was the longest single-line span in Britain – impressive statistics for a footbridge. Keep straight ahead at the far end to rejoin your outward route at a small picnic site. Turn left on the farm road to return to the starting point. ●

Culbin Forest

Start	Wellhill car park, Culbin Forest, 3 miles (4.8km) north-west of Forres
Distance	8½ miles (13.7km)
Approximate time	4 hours
Parking	Wellhill car park
Refreshments	None
Ordnance Survey maps	Landranger 27 (Nairn & Forres), Pathfinder 145, NH96/NJ06 (Findhorn & Culbin Forest)

Until large-scale forestry planting started in the late 1940s, Culbin was a desert of shifting sands, where wind-blown dunes up to 100ft (30m) high covered an area of 9500 acres (3844 ha). The Forestry Commission acquired the Culbin sands in the 1920s and 30s and stabilised the dunes with brushwood before planting them with pine trees. Since then the forest has matured into a unique environment that has been designated both a Forest Nature Reserve and a Site of Special Scientific Interest. This long walk explores the eastern end of the forest and the neighbouring coast, where it borders on Findhorn Bay.

The sands first encroached on the estate of Culbin in the late 17th century, after the coastal dunes had been destabilized by turf-cutting and the pulling of marram grass for thatch. Westerly gales in the autumn of 1694 began the sands' eastward march across Culbin, burying fields and orchards and driving the Laird of Culbin into debt and despair. (In an attempt to regain his fortune, he joined the ill-fated Darien Venture of 1698–1700, and died in the fever-ridden swamps of Central America.)

To aid navigation, most of the road junctions in Culbin Forest are marked with numbered posts; without them, it would be all too easy to get lost. Go through the gate beyond the car park, and turn right at the first junction (no. 43), and right again at the next (no. 2). The forest trees are mostly Scots pine

and Corsican pine, which were found to be most suited to the unusual conditions. Beneath them a carpet of moss and lichen has developed, along with heather in the more open areas.

Two miles (3.2km) further on you reach an information board beside a partially buried tree Ⓐ. The first trees to be planted at Culbin were gradually buried by the shifting sands, but they kept on growing – many of the trees you see here are standing in 10–15ft (3–5m) of sand. Soon after passing the buried tree, the road bends around to the right and reaches junction no. 4 Ⓑ, where the route goes left. At the next fork (junction no. 3) Ⓒ go right, and then 90 degrees left. Another right-angled turn to the left (without a marker post) Ⓓ soon leads to the shore opposite Findhorn village.

Like Culbin, the original Findhorn village fell victim to natural disaster. It was washed away with the shifting gravel spits at the mouth of the river; before 1701, the old village stood about 1 mile (1.6m) to the north-west of the present one, a site that is now covered by the sea. The Findhorn River once reached the sea several miles to the west of this spot, but the migrating dunes dammed the old river mouth and forced it to cut the new outlet that you see today. The tidal inlet of Findhorn Bay is an important wildlife habitat, and is now an RSPB Nature Reserve; as well as the bird life, which includes visiting ospreys in summer and long-tailed ducks in winter, you can see seals hauled out on the sand bars at low water.

Descend to the sandy beach and follow it past the mouth of the bay, then continue west along the shore for nearly 2 miles (3.2km), with views across the firth to the hills of Easter Ross and Sutherland. Here you can see how the sea is eroding the unprotected dunes above the beach, as the process of longshore drift transports the sediment along the coast and deposits it on the sand bars a few miles to the west. After passing a series of dilapidated wooden groynes extending out into the sea, you reach one that runs parallel to the coast. Just beyond it, the trees that have lined

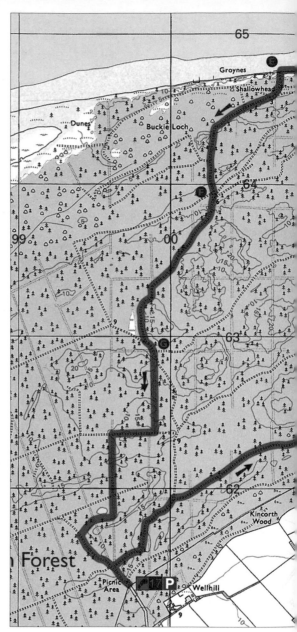

the shore for the past 2 miles (3.2km) thin out – turn left on to a broad sandy path that leads away from the sea over the low, grassy dunes 🅴 towards two ruined sheds in a wide grassy clearing.

Bear right past the sheds, and then turn right along a forestry road at the edge of the trees. The road passes an information board describing Buckie Loch, then turns south and plunges

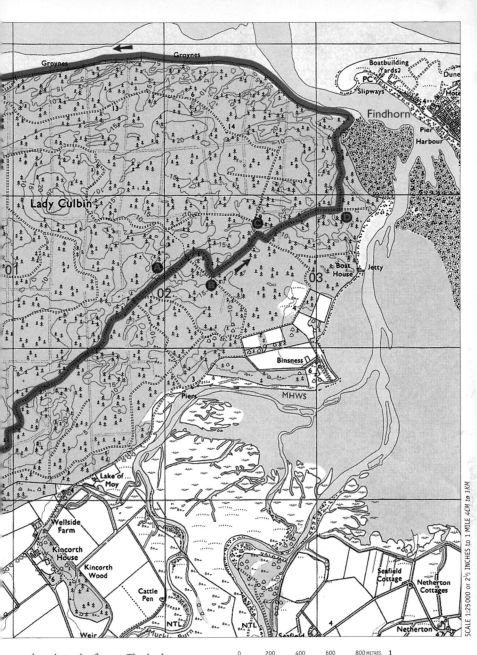

SCALE 1:25000 or 2½ INCHES to 1 MILE 4CM to 1KM

| 0 | 200 | 400 | 600 | 800 METRES | 1 |
| 0 | 200 | 400 | 600 YARDS | ½ | KILOMETRES MILES |

deep into the forest. The loch was once a bog that occupied part of the old channel of the Findhorn River, but it was breached by the sea in 1978 and the salt water has killed off many of the trees and other plants; continuing erosion means that it will probably eventually become salt marsh.

At junction no. 8 ⑧, keep straight ahead. The variety of wildlife that inhabits the forest is impressive, considering that the area was barren dunes a mere 70 years ago. Roe deer, fox, red squirrel and badger can be found, and the forest birds include capercaillie, crested tit and crossbill. The range of insect species, including many kinds of butterflies and spiders, is of national importance (watch out for the monster mosquitoes!). Over 130 species of lichen have been recorded, and in some areas (notably near junction no. 12) lichens make up around 90% of the ground cover.

As you continue through the forest, you join another road which comes in from the right (at junction no. 12), and soon afterwards you arrive at junction no. 9 Ⓖ. Leave the road here, and bear right up a sandy path that follows a fire-break through the trees. At the next road turn right, then go left along the second fire-break you come to (just as the road begins to slope downhill). A broad sandy path runs along the fire-break, and crosses another road at a blue waymark. From this point on, the route follows the blue waymarks as the path curves to the right around a wildlife pond that has been created in an old gravel quarry. After the pond, the path joins a forestry road that leads back to the car park at Wellhill. ●

The beach at Culbin Sands

Big Burn Glen and Ben Bhraggie

Start	Big Burn car park. Turn off the A9 ½ mile (800m) north of Golspie, signposted 'Backies'. The car park is on the left, ½ mile (800m) from the main road
Distance	6 miles (9.7km)
Approximate time	3 hours
Parking	Big Burn car park
Refreshments	Pubs and tearooms in Golspie
Ordnance Survey maps	Landranger 17 (Helmsdale & Strath of Kildonan), Pathfinder 106, NC80/90 (Brora)

Beinn a' Bhragaidh ('the speckled hill', more commonly spelt Ben Bhraggie or Ben Vraggie) is a more prominent landmark than its modest height (1300ft/396m) might suggest, as it rises steeply above the seaside town of Golspie and is topped by a huge 19th-century monument to the first Duke of Sutherland. The normal route direct from Golspie to the summit is short and steep, but this walk follows a longer and more leisurely route up the scenic glen of the Big Burn and around the easier-angled northern side of the hill. Choose a clear day for the ascent, as the views from the top are magnificent.

Go through the small gate at the back of the parking area and turn right along the path signposted with a red arrow towards the waterfall. The route leads through pleasant woods of oak, ash, beech and sycamore and, when the path forks, heads downhill to the left to reach a viewpoint overlooking the cascade. Here the peaty brown waters of the Big Burn tumble over a cliff at the point where the more resistant Old Red Sandstone outcrop that forms Ben Bhraggie is faulted against the younger and softer Jurassic sandstones of the Golspie coast.

Cut back left and continue downhill to an information board beside a wooden footbridge. Don't cross this bridge, but turn right and follow the path upstream along the bank of the burn to a second, metal footbridge and cross there. On the far side, turn right to visit a viewing platform below the waterfall, then return to the bridge and turn right up the steps. The path leads to yet another bridge, this time above the falls. Cross it and turn left along a path that follows the bank of the burn, through a clearing thick with wild raspberries, to a fourth footbridge at a small waterfall.

The path on the far side climbs up leftwards through the trees to reach a stile and kissing-gate at a minor road. Turn left along the road. Soon Ben Bhraggie with its hilltop monument comes into view up ahead to the right, and you arrive at a junction where the road bends 90 degrees to the left Ⓐ. Turn right along an unsurfaced road, past a pretty cottage and through a gate into a forestry plantation of Scots pine. The pleasant, grassy track is fringed with bell heather and ling, and in summer the tiny yellow flowers of tormentil brighten the verge.

At a crossroads in the middle of the forest, keep straight on until the road finally emerges from the trees at a gate and stile. The grassy track now climbs gently across the heather-clad back of Ben Bhraggie, with views of Dunrobin Glen and lonely Loch nan Caorach, before reaching the summit plateau Ⓑ and the huge monument to the Duke of Sutherland. The monument was erected in 1834, and consists of a 30-ft (9m) high statue of the duke set on a 76-ft (23m) high pedestal, and is a prominent landmark for many miles around. The inscription on the front reads 'George Granville, 1st Duke of Sutherland, born 1758, died 1833, of loved, revered and cherished memory, erected by his tenantry and friends', although his

The Sutherland Monument on Ben Bhraggie

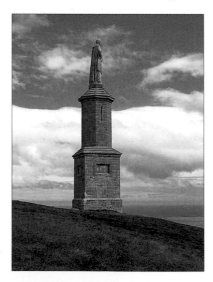

tenantry and their descendants remembered him more for his part in initiating the Highland Clearances.

George Granville Leveson-Gower, Marquess of Stafford, became the largest landowner in Britain when, in 1785, he married Elizabeth Gordon, Countess of Sutherland. Known as the 'Great Improver', his policy of agricultural reform in the Sutherland estates is remembered above all for the brutal eviction of over 5,000 tenants between 1807 and 1821. He was created 1st Duke of Sutherland in 1833, a mere six months before he died. Today, there is a continuing debate as to whether the monument should be removed, and replaced with one that commemorates the evicted crofters.

The view to the south looks over Loch Fleet and the Dornoch Firth to the hills of Easter Ross and the Black Isle, with the long, low finger of Tarbat Ness marking the southern edge of the firth; beyond that you can make out the distant coast near Elgin, and on a good day even the Cairngorms are visible. Turning to the north-east, you can see

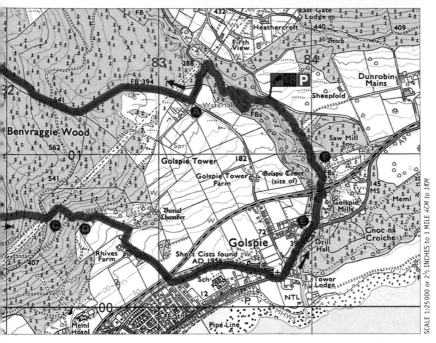

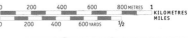

the town of Golspie straggling along the sandy shore, with the pointed turrets of Dunrobin Castle poking above the trees, and the houses of Brora in the distance.

From the monument, take the footpath heading straight down the hillside towards Golspie. The path passes through a gate into the forestry plantation, and descends steeply through the trees. Soon after crossing one forestry road beside a large boulder you reach a second road beneath power lines, at a signpost marked 'BBFP' (for 'Ben Bhraggie Footpath') ●. The path continues on the far side of the road, following the break in the trees beneath the power lines. A short distance beyond the first pylon, the path turns right and heads into the trees, passing more 'BBFP' signs (this is the direct route from Golspie to the monument, and the signs are meant to be seen while heading uphill). When you reach a broader forest trail go left, then straight across a crossroads ●, then left again, all in the space of 100 yds (91m).

The route continues past a gate and some water tanks, then turns right at a farm road, and passes to the left of Rhives Farm before passing under a railway bridge to reach Golspie at a square with a granite fountain dedicated to the first duke's wife Elizabeth, the Duchess-Countess of Sutherland, who died in 1838. Turn left along a minor road, past the school and industrial estate, to reach the main road. Turn left again, past the Sutherland Arms Hotel (the first coaching inn in Sutherland, dating from 1808) and the neighbouring garage ●, then bear left before the bridge through a parking area, at the far end of which is a path signposted 'Waterfall, 20 minutes'. The path crosses the burn and then passes beneath the railway bridge before bearing right, away from the stream, to reach a junction at a low metal post with two yellow arrows and a red one ●. Fork right, up the steep bank, and at the top of the hill turn left on a broader trail which soon leads back to the starting point. ●

Tarbat Ness and Portmahomack

Start	Car park at Tarbat Ness lighthouse, 6 miles (9.7km) east of Tain
Distance	8½ miles (13.7km)
Approximate time	4 hours
Parking	Car park at Tarbat Ness lighthouse
Refreshments	Pub and tearoom in Portmahomack
Ordnance Survey maps	Landranger 21 (Dornoch, Alness & Invergordon area), Pathfinder 124, NH88/98 (Dornoch Firth and Tarbat Ness)

This is a long coastal walk worthy of a full day, with a break for lunch in the pleasant fishing village of Portmahomack. Be sure to bring along your binoculars – in addition to the many species of seabird that frequent the Ness, there is a chance of seeing otters on the west coast of the peninsula near Port Beag and Port Mor. As the route passes through fields which may contain sheep and cattle, dogs should be left at home.

Begin by walking back along the road to a T-junction, then turn left downhill to a stone jetty and slipway. Beyond the hut on the right, a wooden gate gives access to a path along the shore. The path wanders along the grassy raised beach between the high water mark and the steep bluffs of the old sea-cliffs, made of reddish-brown and greenish sandstones of Middle Old Red Sandstone age; one of the outcrops at Rubha na h-Iolaire is marked with vintage graffiti, including the inscription 'JSM PERTH 1912'.

At Tigh na Creige **A**, the raised beach has been eroded away, and while agile walkers can clamber round the point on rocky ledges at low tide, the easier alternative is to detour briefly along the top of the cliffs. Climb up a steep path just before the point and go through a wooden gate at the meeting of three fences. Beyond the gate follow the fence rightwards for 20 yds (18m), then turn left across the top of an earthen bank that dams a small pond. Follow a faint path rightwards along the far side of the pond then, having passed a low grassy knoll on the left, turn left and head towards the sea. An obvious gap between two clumps of gorse leads to the top of a broad, easy-angled shelf that slopes gently back down to the shore.

The path now continues along the foreshore without further incident for 2½ miles (4km), to the village of Rockfield. The straight line of the coast here is controlled geologically by the Great Glen Fault, which extends north-east from Inverness beneath the sea. The sea-cliffs reach their highest point

Tarbat Ness lighthouse

at Creag nan Eun ('bird rock'), a popular seabird nesting site. Further on, you pass beneath Ballone Castle, a Z-plan tower house which was built for the Earl of Ross in the 16th century and is currently being restored as a private dwelling, before reaching the little hamlet of Rockfield ●.

At the edge of the village, turn right up the hill, and follow the minor road across the peninsula towards Portmahomack, with grand views across the Dornoch Firth to the hills of Sutherland. At the T-junction just beyond Highfield farm, continue straight across the green to the bus shelter and turn right along the main street of Portmahomack ●. This picturesque fishing village takes its name from St Colmac, and is noted for Tarbat Old Church, whose unusual domed tower overlooks the bay from a low hilltop, and also for its pleasant sandy beach.

Continue through the village to the harbour (designed by Thomas Telford) with its two old 'girnals', or grain stores, that were once used to store the barley and oats gathered by feudal landowners as payment in kind for agricultural rents. The smaller of the two, with crow-stepped gables, dates from the late 16th century, and the larger one from 1779. Go past the harbour and the parking area beyond it, and then head for a gate that lies between the houses and the shore. A good path leads along the springy turf of the foreshore, with stiles over the first few fences.

The cliffs on this side of the peninsula are composed of younger, orange-red sandstones of Upper Old Red Sandstone age. The rocky foreshore is the haunt of curlews, oystercatchers and herons, and if you are lucky you may see an otter or two, but on weekdays the peace is likely to be disturbed by RAF Tornadoes making low-level approaches to the bombing range at Whiteness Sands near Tain. At Port Mor, about 100 yds (91m) after crossing a rickety wooden gate at the end of a rusty old fence ●, head up right along a broad track through the gorse to the top of the bluffs, and bear left along the edge of a large expanse of gorse to a pair of gates. Go through the left-hand gate, and follow the fence back towards the sea.

The path, though fainter now, still follows the turf above the high-water mark. At Port nan Each ●, it squeezes through a thistly patch between an overgrown pond (used as a rubbish tip by the local farmer) and the sea, and crosses a fence before reaching the windswept, grassy heath of Tarbat Ness. The lighthouse here is the second tallest in the UK, and the point itself is a popular bird-watching venue. In autumn, with onshore winds, gannets, great skuas, and manx and sooty shearwaters can be seen, while in winter keep an eye open for scoters and long-tailed ducks.

Follow the stone wall that surrounds the lighthouse precinct (now a private dwelling) as it runs south-west away from the sea, pass through a gate by a small plantation of trees, and continue to a second gate which leads to the public road. Turn left and left again to return to the car park. ●

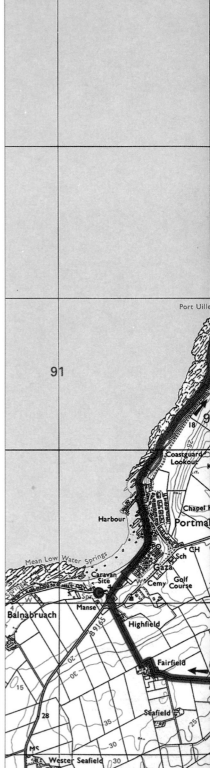

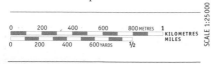

SCALE 1:25000 or 2½ INCHES to 1 MILE 4CM to 1KM

Meallfuarvonie

Start	Grotaig, 4 miles (6.4km) from Drumnadrochit at end of minor road to Bunloit
Distance	6 miles (9.7km)
Approximate time	3 hours
Parking	Car park on right side of road, 100 yds (91m) before start of path
Refreshments	None
Ordnance Survey maps	Landranger 26 (Inverness & Strathglass area), Pathfinder 208, NH42/52 (Mid Loch Ness)

Meallfuarvonie or Meall Fuar-mhonaidh (the name means 'rounded hill of the cold moor') is the highest point on the northern shore of Loch Ness, and provides magnificent views along the entire length of the Great Glen. It is an easy walk, on grass and heather, and the starting point high above the loch leaves only a relatively short climb to the 2293ft (699m) summit. However, in poor visibility it is possible to become disoriented on the summit plateau, so a map and compass should be carried.

The well-signposted path to Meallfuarvonie begins at a small bridge at the very end of the minor road from Drumnadrochit to Bunloit, just before the pottery. Go through the gate to the right of the bridge, and follow the path along the burn to the birch woods. Signposts direct you through the woods as the path swings right and begins to head uphill along the side of a small gorge, crossing several stiles, to emerge on to the open heather moorland.

The path is well-trodden, but its route is also clearly marked by a couple of timber posts as it climbs to the crest of the hill's north-east ridge at a high deer fence Ⓐ. Cross the stile and follow the delightful ridge crest for almost 2 miles (3.2km), mainly on springy heather with the occasional boggy section.

There are four cairns on the summit plateau, the furthest away of which is

the true summit Ⓑ. There are spectacular views along the Great Glen in both directions, and west to the mountains of Glen Affric and Kintail. On the opposite shore of Loch Ness lies the village of Foyers, with Loch Mhor

above and Farigaig Forest and Dùn Dearduil (see Walk 13) to its left. Beyond rises the high, featureless tableland of the Monadhliath. At your feet is the plateau known as Lòn na Fola ('the bloody meadow'), the site of a clan battle between Macdonalds and Mackenzies in 1603.

The Great Glen, which runs for 55 miles (88km) from Fort William to Inverness, has been eroded along the line of the Great Glen Fault, a major fracture in the Earth's crust. A zone of crushed and shattered rock caused by repeated earth movements has been gouged out by glaciers, so that the floor of the glen is nowhere more than 130ft (39m) above sea level – indeed, the bottom of Loch Ness is more than 600ft (183m) *below* sea level – while the sides of the glen rise steeply to more than 900ft (274m).

The 19th-century geologist Hugh Miller described the Great Glen (also known as Glen Mor or Glen Albyn) as 'a foot track, hollowed by the frequent tread of earthquakes to mark the course

Looking south along the Great Glen from Meallfuarvonie

in which they journeyed'. Inverness suffered serious damage from the earthquakes of 13 August 1816 and 18 September 1901, and the Great Glen Fault is still the most seismically active in Britain. When the Kessock Bridge was built in 1980, it incorporated huge foundations and hydraulic buffers to protect it against earthquakes.

Return to the car park by the same route, remembering to take the left-hand fork in the path when you reach the top of the birch woods. ●

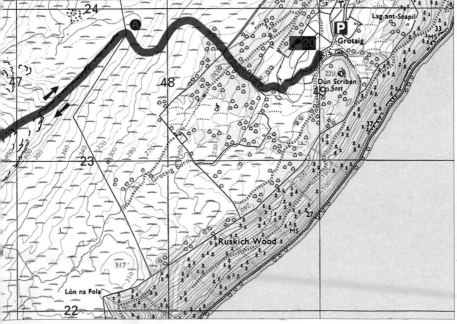

Ben Rinnes

Start	Minor road off the B9009, 4 miles (6.4km) south-west of Dufftown
Distance	4½ miles (7.2km)
Approximate time	3 hours
Parking	Roadside parking at start (do not block gate)
Refreshments	None
Ordnance Survey maps	Landranger 28 (Elgin, Dufftown & surrounding area), Pathfinder 196, NJ23/33 (Glen Fiddich)

Ben Rinnes (2756ft/840m) rises to the south of the Spey valley at Charlestown of Aberlour, its foothills fringed with whisky distilleries. It is the highest summit between the Cairngorms and the Moray Firth, and on a clear day the views are superb. Although its ascent is an easy one for experienced hillwalkers, less hardy hikers will find it a long, tiring climb, and the summit can be cold and windy even in summer, so come prepared with proper walking boots, warm clothes and waterproofs.

Ben Rinnes is part of the walker-friendly Glenlivet Estates, and an information board describing the route to the summit has been erected at the start of the walk. Navigation is not difficult – there is only one path, and it follows the crest of the east ridge all the way to the top. The first part of the walk is on a 4-wheel drive track that zigzags up to the top of Round Hill 🅐, then continues through a gate and on up the easier-angled ridge ahead. The views now begin to open up, with the rounded

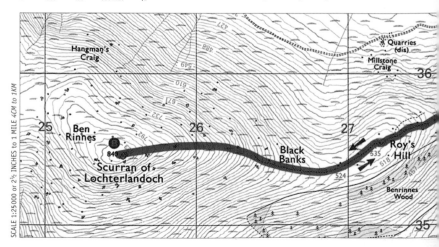

bulk of Ben Avon and the Cairngorms rising on the southern horizon, and the fertile Laich of Moray spreading north to the coast. Ahead rises the summit, crowned by the rugged granite tors called the Scurran of Lochterlandoch.

Beyond the top of Roy's Hill the well-trodden path continues through the

The clear path up the east ridge of Ben Rinnes

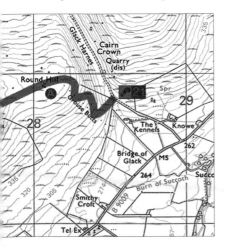

peat hags of the Black Banks and up the final 1000ft (305m) grind over heather and broken rock to the wrinkled granite tors of the summit ⬤. The panorama to the north extends over the valley of the Spey and the lowlands around Elgin to the distant shores of the Moray Firth. North-west lie the mountains of Easter Ross and Inverness-shire, while to the south-west the high plateau of the Cairngorms fills the horizon. Return by the same route.

If you feel like reviving yourself with a drop of the hard stuff after the climb, you need not look too far afield. The Glenfarclas, Glenlivet, Glenfiddich, Tamnavulin and Cardhu distilleries are all within 20 minutes' drive of Ben Rinnes, and all offer guided tours which include either a nip or a miniature to take away. ⬤

Loch Affric

Start	River Affric car park, at end of public road up Glen Affric, 10 miles (16.1km) south-west of Cannich
Distance	11 miles (17.7km)
Approximate time	5½ hours
Parking	River Affric car park
Refreshments	None
Ordnance Survey maps	Landranger 25 (Glen Carron), Pathfinder 206, NH02/12 (Loch Affric) and 207, NH22/32 (Tomich)

Glen Affric is one of Scotland's most scenic valleys, with glittering lochs, rugged mountains, and one of Britain's largest surviving native pine forests. This circuit of Loch Affric follows part of the classic cross-country walking route from Cannich to Kintail, visiting the remote and beautiful upper glen, before returning through the Caledonian pine forest on the south shore of the loch. Though long, the walk is on good paths and forestry roads, and involves very little ascent.

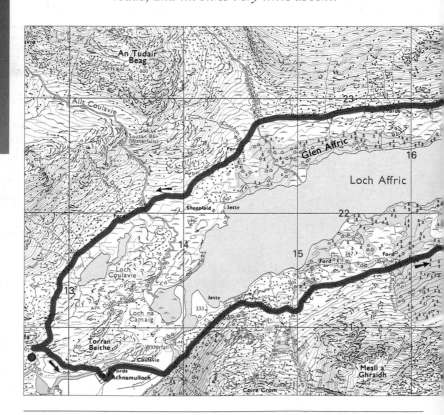

Glen Affric is not only picturesque – it is also a haven for wildlife, including deer, pine marten, red squirrel, otter, golden eagle and wildcat. The pine forests are home to capercaillie, black grouse, crossbill, crested tit, redpoll and siskin (the latter two more common in winter), and both red-throated and black-throated divers can be seen on the lochs. Glen Affric is also one of the few places in the UK where you can see the rare northern emerald dragonfly (*Somatochlora arctica*). This beautiful insect, with its dark, metallic green-bronze thorax, is found only in the north-west Highlands.

Walk back out of the car park towards the road and turn left along its unsurfaced continuation (though marked 'Authorised vehicles only', it is a pedestrian route). After almost 1 mile

(1.6km), you reach the Keeper's House at the gate to Affric Lodge ●; here the route bears to the right along a good footpath signposted 'Kintail and Hostel Route'. The walk follows the north side of Loch Affric for about 4 miles (6.4km), and offers fairly easy going on a well-made path.

The path keeps fairly high above the loch, with views ahead to the shapely peak of Mullach Fraoch-choire. Beyond it, the River Affric rises on the northern slopes of Beinn Fhada in Kintail, less than 6 miles (9.7km) from the west coast, and flows almost all the way across the country, merging with the rivers Glass and Beauly to reach the east coast at the Beauly Firth near Inverness.

After passing little Loch Coulavie, the path makes a short climb before dropping down rightwards to meet the track from Athnamulloch bothy to Kintail ●. Turn left on to this track to head back towards Loch Affric, and

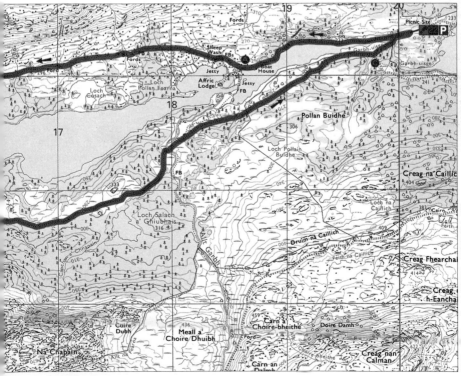

cross the bridge. On the far side of the river lies the white cottage of Athnamulloch and a couple of abandoned croft buildings, with a Forest Enterprise information board.

Turn left at the cottage and follow the forestry road that leads along the south side of the loch for 5 miles (8km), with good views across the loch to the high summits of Mam Sodhail and Carn Eighe, and the dark, conical peak of An Tudair Beag towering above the Sputan Ban waterfall. Towards the east end of the loch, the road passes through attractive woods of native Scots pine.

There is only one junction on this road ⓒ, and it lies only a short distance from the end of the walk. Take the left fork, which leads through a gate, across the river and back to the car park. ●

Looking towards Kintail from upper Glen Affric

Ben Griam Beg

Start	A897 Helmsdale to Thurso road, 4 miles (6.4km) north of Kinbrace
Distance	9 miles (14.5km)
Approximate time	5 hours
Parking	Space for two cars at deserted Ballach Cottage, 200 yds (183m) north of start
Refreshments	None
Ordnance Survey maps	Landrangers 10 (Strathnaver) and 17 (Helmsdale & Strath of Kildonan), Pathfinders 65, NC84/94 (Forsinard) and 76, NC83/93 (Kinbrace)

Ben Griam Mór and Ben Griam Beg rise in splendid isolation above the desolate moors of eastern Sutherland. Both peaks can be climbed from the Garvault Hotel on the Kinbrace to Bettyhill road, but this walk takes the direct route to the summit of Ben Griam Beg (1902ft/580m), the more interesting of the two hills. Not for the inexperienced, this is a long and tiring walk in a very remote area, so take full hill-walking equipment and be sure to notify someone of your intended route. See pages 14, 92 and 93 for walking safety information. In the stalking season (especially mid-August to mid-October), contact Achentoul Estate, Tel. 01431 831227, to see if shooting is taking place on the hill.

Start at the unsurfaced private road that leaves the west side of the A897 about 200 yds (183m) south of Ballach Cottage, and follow it across the railway and past the north end of Loch an Ruathair to its end at the estate cottage at Greamachary Ⓐ. The scenery is wild and desolate, but occasionally ospreys

Ben Griam Mór (left) and Ben Griam Beg

can be seen hunting for fish over the loch. The name 'Griam' derives either from the Gaelic for 'lichen-covered' or from the Norse for 'dark and massive', and your interpretation will probably depend on the weather – on a sunny summer's day there is a grand feeling of spaciousness and light, but in dull weather the word 'grim' springs all too readily to mind.

Follow the north bank of the Greamachary Burn for a way until you can strike northward up the heather-covered hillside towards the eastern shoulder of Ben Griam Beg. There is no path, and the going is rough and boggy at first, but becomes firmer as the slope

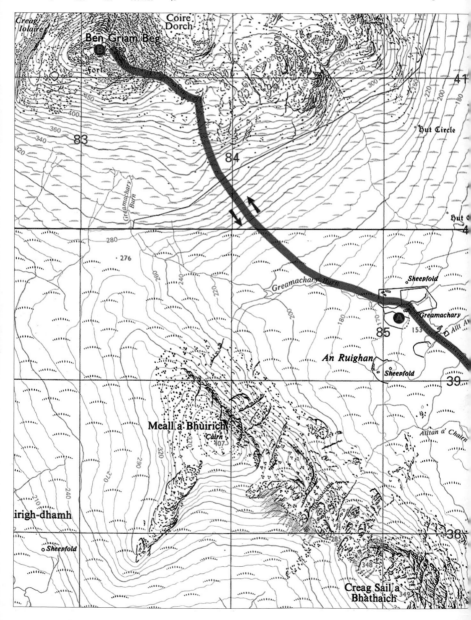

steepens. From the shoulder, climb more steeply up the final eastern ridge to the triangulation pillar at the summit ⓑ.

The panoramic view from the top is superb, with the Orkney islands clearly visible about 40 miles (64km) away to the north-east. The summit is occupied by the remains of the highest hill-fort in Scotland – drystone walls about 6ft (2m) thick enclose an area about 500ft by 200ft (152m by 61m), with the entrance on the north side. It is thought that the fort is early Bronze Age rather than Iron Age, dating from before 1500 BC. The hill is also a Site of Special Scientific Interest, noted for its communities of arctic-alpine plants – a good indication of the typical weather conditions on the summit. Return to the start by the same route.　　　　●

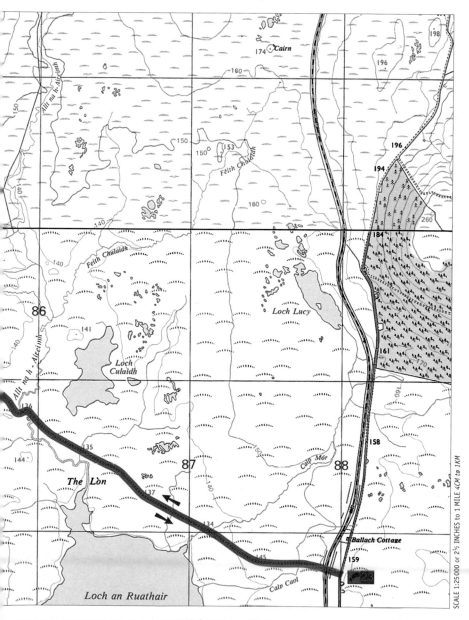

SCALE 1:25 000 or 2½ INCHES to 1 MILE 4CM to 1KM

The Glen Loth Hills

Start	Bridge over Sletdale Burn in Glen Loth. Turn off A9 at Lothbeg, 5 miles (8km) north of Brora, on a steep, single-track road, and follow it for 2 miles (3.2km) to the bridge
Distance	6½ miles (10.5km)
Approximate time	4 hours
Parking	Space for one car on right side of road immediately after bridge
Refreshments	None
Ordnance Survey maps	Landranger 17 (Helmsdale & Strath of Kildonan), Pathfinder 96, NC81/91 (Beinn Dhorain)

Lonely Glen Loth lies only a few miles off the busy A9 road to Wick, but it feels much more isolated. The easily defended glen was once a centre of Iron Age occupation, as witnessed by the many archaeological remains, and was later home to several crofts, but it has been deserted for many decades and the crumbling cottages and sheepfolds simply add to the air of desolation. This route climbs the heathery hills on the west side of the glen, which afford fine views over the eastern seaboard of Sutherland and Caithness. During the stalking season (especially mid-August to mid-October), contact Kildonan Estate, Tel. 01431 831263, before venturing on to the hills. See pages 14, 92 and 93 for walking safety information.

Cross the fence on the west side of the road at the cattle-grid just north of the bridge, and climb up to the top of the steep bank on the north side of the Sletdale Burn, where you will find two prominent standing stones, about 6ft (2m) tall. A narrow path heads up the valley, but ignore it and head towards the broad heathery ridge that climbs gently to Druim Dearg (1459ft/444m). The hillside is heathery but not too steep, and it is possible to link sheep tracks together to give easier walking.

From the cairn on the summit of Druim Dearg Ⓐ, follow a faint track north-west to the saddle below Beinn

Dhorain before making the final 600ft (183m) climb to the top. A dip of only 100ft (30m) and a further ½ mile (800m) of walking lead to the triangulation pillar atop Ben Uarie (2045ft/623m) Ⓑ. The view north-east extends over the Strath of Kildonan, site of the famous Sutherland Gold Rush of 1868–9, to the pointed summit of Morven and the peat bogs of the Caithness Flow Country, with the twin peaks of Ben Griam Mor and Ben Griam Beg (see Walk 23) rising from the moors

0	200	400	600	800 METRES	1
					KILOMETRES
					MILES
0	200	400	600 YARDS	½	

HEIGHTS SHOWN IN FEET ON THIS MAP EXTRACT

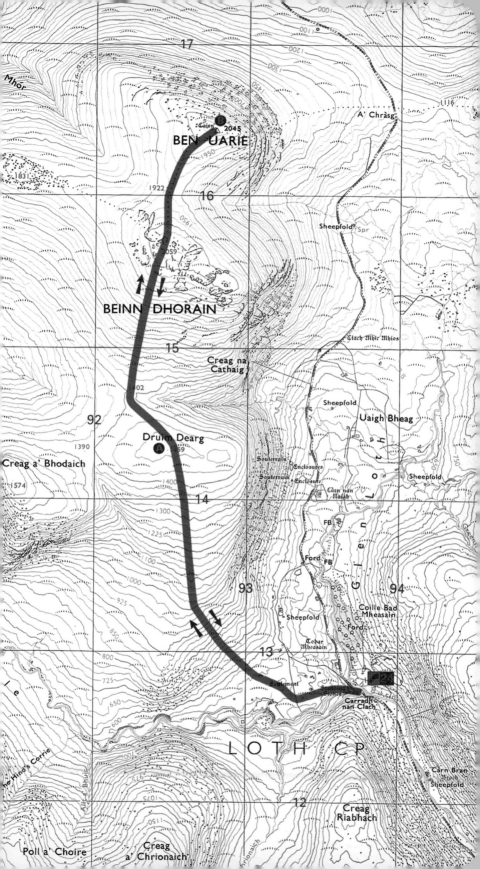

to the north. To the west lies the massive hulk of Ben Klibreck (see Walk 27), and on a clear day you can see the distant peaks of Ben Hope and Ben Loyal to its right.

Return along the ridge and descend by the same route. Don't be tempted to descend early from the hills to the Glen Loth road – not only are these eastern slopes dangerously steep, but there is a high deer fence barring access from the hill on to the road.

Glen Loth

Morven

Start	Braemore, 6 miles (9.7km) east of Dunbeath at end of minor road
Distance	10 miles (16.1km)
Approximate time	6 hours
Parking	Beside the telephone box at Braemore
Refreshments	None
Ordnance Survey maps	Landranger 17 (Helmsdale & Strath of Kildonan), Pathfinders 77, ND03/13 (Latheron) and 87, ND02/12 (Berriedale)

The shapely cone of Morven (2316ft/706 m) is the highest summit in Caithness, and a distinctive landmark that is visible from most parts of the county. Its ascent involves a long and tiring walk, but the effort is rewarded with superb views and a real sense of isolation. This walk takes you into the heart of a very remote area, so go prepared with plenty of food and water. As usual in this kind of terrain, you should inform someone of your intended route and time of return, and the estate requests that you also leave a note of your route at the keeper's cottage. During the stalking season, contact the Braemore Estate keeper, tel. 01593 731371, to check if there is any shooting taking place. See pages 14, 92 and 93 for walking safety information.

Cross the bridge over the Berriedale Water and walk along the road towards Braemore Lodge. At the lodge gate go left (signposted 'Braemore Keeper and Kennels'), and follow the road to the keeper's cottage. Having left a note of your route, go through an unlocked gate onto the moorland beyond. There are fine views south to the craggy peak of Maiden Pap and ahead to the tors of Smean and the distant, volcano-like cone of Morven. The estate road continues for just over 2 miles (3.2km) to the bothy at Corrichoich.

From the bothy, continue along the south bank of the Berriedale Water for about 500 yds (457m) to a grassy knoll topped with the remains of an Iron Age

'wheel-house' Ⓐ. These circular buildings with their radiating internal 'spokes' date from around the 1st century BC to the 2nd century AD, and are confined mostly to Shetland and the Outer Hebrides. This one is much ruined, but you can make out the circular walls, about 60ft (18m) in diameter, with the entrance on the south-east side, and the remains of some of the pillars inside. The valley of the Berriedale Water south-east of Scaraben is rich in prehistoric remains, including burial cairns, hut circles and brochs, and was obviously a major centre of Iron Age settlement.

Strike south-west along the south side of the Allt Coire Riabhaich burn

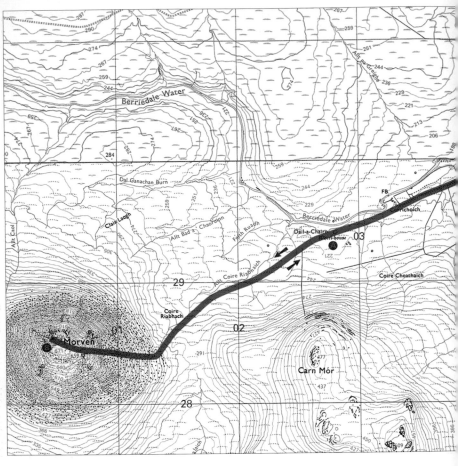

| 0 | 200 | 400 | 600 | 800 METRES | 1 |
| 0 | 200 | 400 | 600 YARDS | ½ | |

towards the saddle beneath the eastern
flank of Morven, whose conical outline
now dominates the view. There is no
obvious path, and the going is rough
and occasionally boggy.

From the saddle it is a hard grind of
1300ft (396 m) up scree and steep,
heather-clad slopes to the gnarled tors
that decorate the summit ⓑ. The peak
is composed of Old Red Sandstone
conglomerate, which contains
fragments of older basement rocks such
as granite, quartzite and schist; the tors
of neighbouring Smean and the peak of
Maiden Pap which you passed on the
way are formed of the same rock. In

contrast, the rounded, humpback ridge
of Scaraben to the south-east has been
carved from an outcrop of more evenly-
weathered quartzite.

The views from the summit are
superb – west and north-west to the
mountains of Sutherland, notably Ben
Klibreck (see Walk 27), Ben Hope and
Ben Loyal, and the twin summits of Ben
Griam Mor and Ben Griam Beg (see
Walk 23); north and north-east over the
dark peat-bogs and forestry plantations
of the Flow Country to the distant
Orkney Islands; and south across the
Moray Firth to the faint blue smudge on
the horizon that is the Cairngorms,
almost 80 miles (128km) away.

Return to the start by the same route,
and inform the keeper of your return. ●

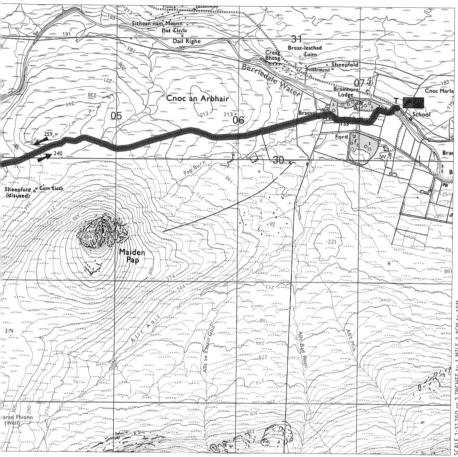

The conical Old Red Sandstone peaks of Maiden Pap (left) and Morven

Ben Wyvis

Start	400 yds (366m) south of Garbat, on the A835 from Garve to Ullapool
Distance	8 miles (12.9km)
Approximate time	5 hours
Parking	Unmarked parking area at start, with space for 8 cars. Larger lay-by at Garbat
Refreshments	None
Ordnance Survey maps	Landranger 20 (Beinn Dearg), Pathfinder 143, NH46/56 (Ben Wyvis)

The name 'Wyvis' probably derives from a Gaelic word that translates as 'enormous', and the great bulk of Ben Wyvis certainly dominates the landscape for many miles around. It is not a shapely mountain, and the ascent is straightforward if rather dull, but it is worthwhile for the grand views of the North East Highlands, and for the rare alpine plants that grow on the summit plateau. Ben Wyvis is a Munro (a peak of 3000ft/914m or more) so follow the walking safety guidelines on pages 14, 92 and 93.

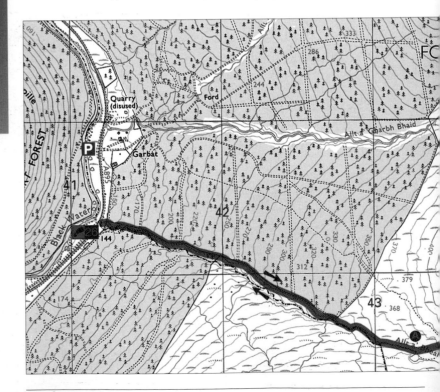

On the north side of the bridge where the A835 Garve to Ullapool road crosses the Allt a' Bhealaich Mhoir a signpost marks the start of the Ben Wyvis footpath. The well-made path, which has been improved by the work of the Ross and Cromarty Footpath Trust, climbs up the true right bank of the burn for just over 1 mile (1.6km) to a large wooden gate at the upper limit of the forestry plantation.

Beyond the gate, an information board welcomes you to the Ben Wyvis National Nature Reserve. The path, now soft and peaty, continues along the banks of the burn, while the steep, angular shoulder of An Cabar, the south-western extremity of the Ben Wyvis summit ridge, rises steeply on the left. 200 yds (183m) beyond the gate, where the burn loops away from the path **A**, strike up to the left to begin climbing the west ridge of An Cabar. The path is poorly defined to begin with, but it becomes more distinct as you gain height, zigzagging steeply up the ridge crest to arrive at a couple of cairns **B**.

From An Cabar the route lies north along the broad, whaleback summit ridge of Ben Wyvis, and an easy walk of 1½ miles (2.4km) over mossy turf leads to the triangulation pillar (3432ft/1046m) **C**. This high plateau, covered in thin, mossy turf, is the haunt of ptarmigan, dotterel, and mountain hare; botanists should look out for rare alpine plants such as alpine lady's-mantle, and the tiny pink flowers of creeping azalea.

The shaded corries on the eastern flank of the mountain hold their snow well into the summer, a meteorological curiosity which for centuries allowed the Munros of Foulis Castle (near Evanton) to keep their lands, as it was a condition of their tenure that the king

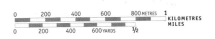

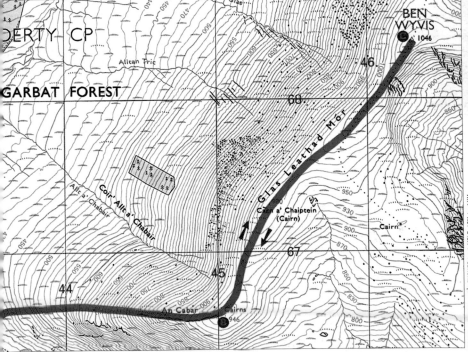

be presented with a snowball whenever he visited. More recently, this feature inspired an ambitious scheme to develop the mountain as a ski resort, complete with a rack railway running from Strathpeffer to the summit; fortunately, however, the plan was never acted on.

The views on a clear day are impressive, encompassing the whole of northern Scotland from the North Sea to the Atlantic, and from Ben Klibreck and Ben Hope to the Cairngorms. Return by the same route. ●

An Cabar – en route to the summit of Ben Wyvis

Ben Klibreck

Start	A836, 4½ miles (7.2km) south of Altnaharra
Distance	7 miles (11.3km)
Approximate time	5 hours
Parking	Roadside parking area at start
Refreshments	None
Ordnance Survey maps	Landranger 16 (Lairg, Loch Shin & surrounding area), Pathfinders 74, NC43/53 (Altnaharra) and 84, NC42/52 (Glen Fiag)

Ben Klibreck (3153ft/961m) is a massive and rather inelegant hill, but like just about every high summit in Sutherland it provides a magnificent viewpoint. The mountain presents its most pleasing profile to the traveller approaching from the south along Strath Vagastie, from which direction the pointed summit cone of Meall nan Con is prominent. This walk takes the most direct route from the road to the summit, and involves a long, steep and tiring climb, one to be undertaken only by fit and experienced hill-walkers – see pages 14, 92 & 93 for walking safety information. During the stalking season, check with the landowners before venturing on to the hill. The lower part of the route (as far as Loch nan Uan) crosses the Altnaharra Estate (tel. 01549 411220); the remainder lies within the Clebrig Farm Estate (tel. 01549 411251).

Cross the River Vagastie at the stepping stones below the parking area, and head diagonally leftward up the hillside, aiming in the general direction of the summit of Ben Klibreck. (If the river is in spate, there is a wooden footbridge about ¾ mile (1.2km) upstream, but there is very limited parking here.) At the top of the first rise, follow the fence leftwards to a gate ● and pass through, then head across boggy ground (rich in insectivorous sundew plants) towards the south end of Loch na Glas-choille. There is only the faintest of trails here, but the path becomes more defined as you follow the fence that runs up the

hillside from Loch na Glas-choille to Loch nan Uan.

When you reach Loch nan Uan, cross the fence to the left and pick up the

Meall nan Con, the highest peak of Ben Klibreck

path that can be seen rising rightwards across the hillside on the far side of the loch. This leads to a large grassy patch amongst the heather 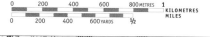, between two small water-courses that fall straight down the steep hillside above. From here it is a hard grind straight uphill for 1000ft (305m), following one of the many faint paths that zigzag up the slope. (If visibility is poor, make a note of the point where you arrive on the ridge ●, so that you can recognise it on the way down. At the time of writing, it is marked by a rusty iron gate propped against a boulder, with an old fence post pointing the way downhill.)

Turn left along the ridge and follow it to the summit cone of Meall nan Con, where a final climb of 660ft (200m) over stony and mossy slopes leads to the triangulation pillar and the crinkled, mica-schist crags of the summit ●. A little way beyond the summit, on the south-east side of the ridge, is the ruin of a tiny bothy which can provide some welcome shelter on a windy day.

Those who think that 'Klibreck' comes from the Gaelic *cliath bhreac*, 'speckled slope or cliff', maintain that the spotty, schistose rocks give the mountain its name, but a Norse derivation is more likely, from *klif brekka*, 'the cliff slope', which well describes Ben Klibreck's massive western flank. The view is as good as one would expect from such an isolated peak, taking in all of Sutherland and the hills of Caithness. Return to the start by the same route. ●

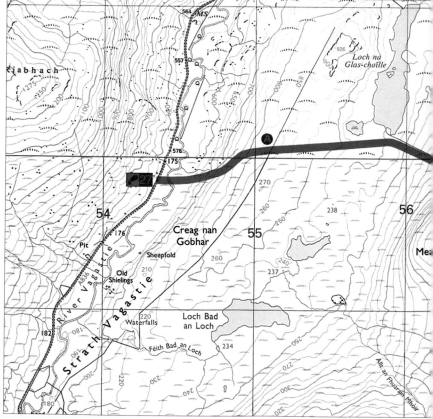

The massive bulk of Ben Klibreck, seen from the south

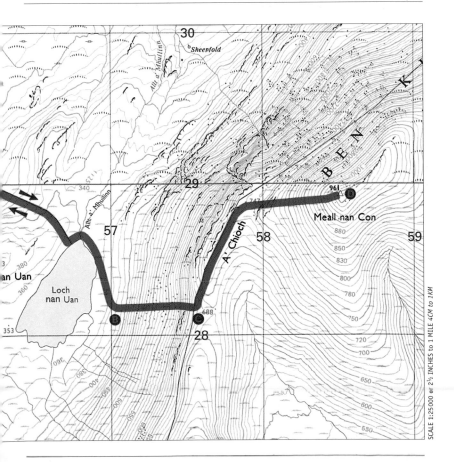

Wade's Road to the Corrieyairack Pass

Start	Minor road to Ardachy, off the A82 near Fort Augustus
Distance	14 miles (22.5km)
Approximate time	7 hours
Parking	1 mile (1.6km) south of Fort Augustus, on the A82 towards Fort William, a minor road branches left, signposted 'Ardachy'. About 300 yds (274m) along, on the right, is a gate with a signpost 'Wade's Road to Laggan'. On the left is parking space for two cars. Otherwise, nearest parking is in Fort Augustus
Refreshments	Hotels and tearooms in Fort Augustus
Ordnance Survey maps	Landranger 34 (Fort Augustus & Glen Albyn area), Pathfinders 238, NH20/30 (Fort Augustus & Loch Garry); 251, NN29/39 (Laggan (Highland); and 252, NN49/59 (Corrieyairack Forest)

The route from Fort Augustus across the Corrieyairack Pass to Dalwhinnie was the last and most challenging of the 18th-century military roads to be built by General George Wade. This walk follows Wade's road to the summit of the pass, a long and tiring expedition, but it can be cut short at any point by simply retracing your steps. Those planning to go all the way to the top should carry full hill-walking equipment – see pages 14, 92 & 93 for walking safety information. Navigation is not a problem on this walk – simply follow the road. At the few places near the start where there might be any doubt as to the route, Scottish Rights of Way Society signposts will keep you right.

Go through the gate and climb steeply up the hillside. This part of the route, immediately above the starting point, is so badly eroded that it looks more like a stream-bed than a road; indeed erosion has become such a problem that the road has been scheduled as an ancient monument and is protected by law – it is an offence to damage the road or its bridges in any way. This has recently caused some friction with the off-road driving fraternity, who want to continue to exercise their right to drive over the pass.

The road was built in 1731 to link Fort Augustus with Dalwhinnie, 22 miles (35km) distant, on the existing military road from Stirling to Inverness. It was constructed of packed boulders and broken stone topped with gravel, with drainage ditches on either side (the

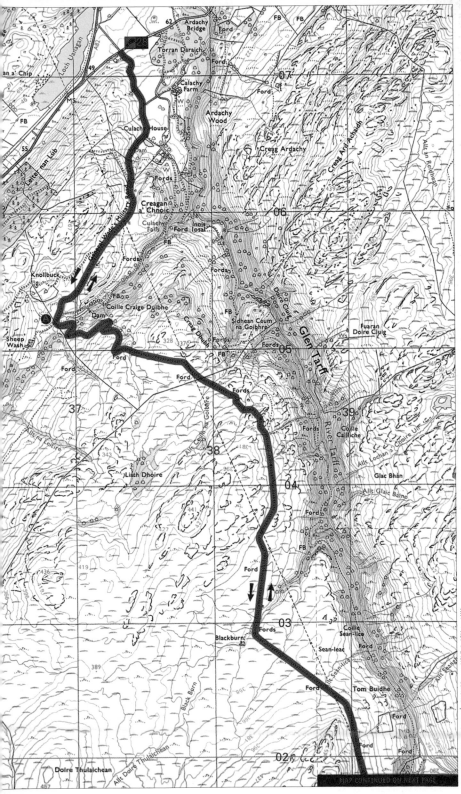

SCALE 1:27777 or about 2½ INCHES to 1 MILE 3.6CM to 1KM

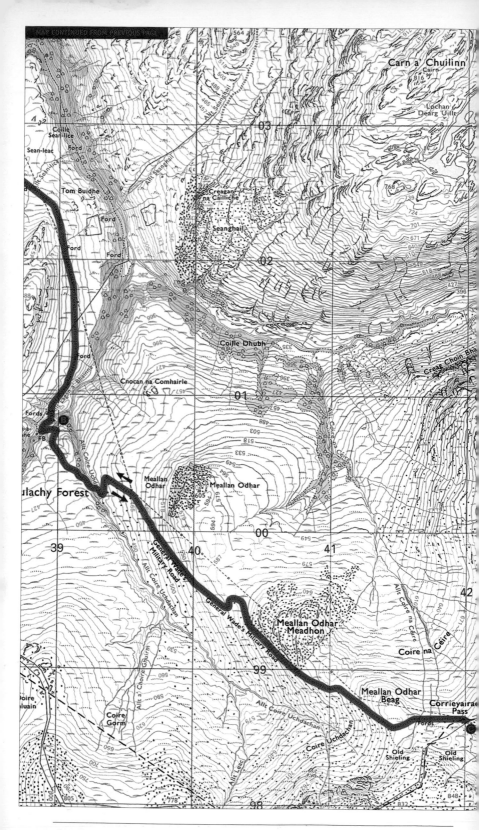

gravel has long since washed away). It was the highest and most difficult of Wade's roads, reaching an altitude of over 2500ft (762m), and required many traverses (zigzags) and retaining walls, especially on the steep slope of Corrieyairack where 18 traverses were originally built.

Wade's soldiers were employed in working parties of 100 men, each party supervised by a captain, two subalterns, two sergeants, two corporals and a drummer. The working season ran from April to October, and at the height of the summer around 500 soldiers would be engaged in road building, while skilled civilian masons worked on the bridges and retaining walls.

After the initial climb past Culachy House the road runs level for ¹/₂ mile (800m) to the bridge on the Connachie Burn , and then begins to switchback up the steep hillside above. Do not cut corners on the zigzags above the bridge, as this only helps to increase erosion. On this section of the road there are several places where you can see the original packed stones laid by General Wade's work parties over 250 years ago.

Just over 4 miles (6.4km) from the start, the road drops into the attractive wooded glen of the Allt Lagan a' Bhainne, where you will find a good picnic spot on a grassy sward beside the river at the bailey bridge ⬤, built in 1961 to replace its 18th-century predecessor. This sheltered nook was christened 'Snugburgh' by Wade's soldiers, and it was here, on 30 October 1732 (the King's birthday), that he

General Wade's bridge over Allt Coire Uchdachan

treated them to a feast of roasted oxen to celebrate the completion of the road.

The piers of Wade's original bridge over the Allt Lagan a' Bhainne lie a short distance upstream, but you can admire a surviving Wade original at the next stream crossing, where the 250-year-old bridge looks sturdier and more secure than its modern replacement. A final few zigzags and a long traverse lead to the broad shoulder of Carn Leac and the summit of the pass, at a height of 2552ft (778m).

A little further on is a linesman's hut ⬤, from which you can look down into the steep bowl of Corrieyairack itself towards the headwaters of the Spey. ('Corrieyairack' is an anglicised version of the Gaelic *coire dearg*, 'the red corrie'.) Ironically, although the road was built to help government troops resist the threat of Jacobite rebellion, it was first used for military purposes by the army of Bonnie Prince Charlie as it marched south to Edinburgh in 1745.

On the long march back to Fort Augustus, you can enjoy magnificent views across the Great Glen, north to Loch Ness and the rounded hump of Meallfuarvonie (see Walk 20), and south to the conical peak of Ben Tee. ⬤

Further Information

The Law and Tradition as they affect Walking in Scotland

Walkers following the routes given in this book should not run into problems, but it is as well to know something about the law as it affects access, and also something of the traditions which can be quite different in Scotland from elsewhere in Britain. Most of this comes down to common sense, observing the country code and having consideration for other people and their activities which, after all, may be their livelihood.

It is often said that there is no law of trespass in Scotland. In fact there is, but the trespass itself is not usually a criminal offence. You can be asked to leave any property, and technically 'reasonable force' may be used to obtain your compliance – though the term is not defined! You can be charged with causing damage due to the trespass, but this would be hard to establish if you were just walking on open, wild, hilly country where, whatever the law, in practice there has been a long tradition of free access for recreational walking – something both the Scottish Landowners' Federation and the Mountaineering Council of Scotland do not want to see changed.

There are certain restrictions. Walkers should obey the country code and seasonal restrictions arising from lambing or stalking. Where there is any likelihood of such restrictions this is mentioned in the text and visitors are asked to comply. When camping, use a campsite. Camp fires should not be lit; they are a danger to moorland and forest, and really not necessary as lightweight and efficient stoves are now available.

Many of the walks in this book are on rights of way. The watchdog on rights of way in Scotland is the Scottish Rights of Way Society (SRWS), who maintain details on all established cases and will, if need be, contest attempted closures. They produce a booklet on the Scottish legal position (Rights of Way, A Guide to the Law in Scotland, 1991), and their green signposts are a familiar sight by many footpaths and tracks, indicating the lines of historic routes.

In Scotland rights of way are not marked on Ordnance Survey maps as is the case south of the border. It was not felt necessary to show these as such on the maps – a further reflection of the freedom to roam that is enjoyed in Scotland. So a path on a map is no indication of a right of way, and many paths and tracks of great use to walkers were built by estates as stalking paths or for private access. While you may traverse such paths, taking due care to avoid damage to property and the natural environment, you should obey restricted access notices and leave if asked to do so.

The only established rights of way are those where a court case has resulted in a legal judgment, but there are thousands of other 'claimed' rights of way. Local planning authorities have a duty to protect rights of way – no easy task with limited resources. Many attempts at closing claimed rights of way have been successfully contested in the courts by the Scottish Rights of Way Society and local authorities.

A dog on a lead or under control may also be taken on a right of way. There is little chance of meeting a free-range solitary bull on any of the walks, and although any herds seen are unlikely to be dairy cattle, all cows can be inquisitive and may approach walkers, especially if they have a dog. Dogs running among stock may be shot on the spot; this is not draconian legislation but a desperate attempt to stop sheep and lambs being harmed, driven to panic or lost, sometimes with fatal results. Any practical points or restrictions applicable will be made in the text of each walk. If there is no comment it can be assumed that the route carries no real restrictions.

Athnamulloch bothy at the head of Glen Affric

Scotland in fact likes to keep everything as natural as possible, so, for instance, waymarking is kept to a minimum (the Scottish Rights of Way Society signposts and Forest Walk markers are in unobtrusive colours). In Scotland people are asked to 'walk softly in the wilderness, to take nothing except photographs, and leave nothing except footprints' – which is better than any law.

Scotland's Hills and Mountains: a Concordat on Access

This remarkable agreement was published early in 1996 and is likely to have considerable influence on walkers' rights in Scotland in the future. The signatories include organisations which have formerly been at odds - the Scottish Landowners' Federation and the Ramblers' Association, for example. However they joined with others to make the Access Forum (a full list of signatories is detailed below). The RSPB and the National Trust

for Scotland did not sign the Concordat initially but it is hoped that they will support its principles.

The signatories of the Concordat are:

Association of Deer Management Groups
Convention of Scottish Local Authorities
Mountaineering Council of Scotland
National Farmers' Union of Scotland
Ramblers' Association Scotland
Scottish Countryside Activities Council
Scottish Landowners' Federation
Scottish Natural Heritage
Scottish Sports Association
Scottish Sports Council

They agreed that the basis of access to the hills for the purposes of informal recreation should be:

Freedom of access exercised with responsibility and subject to reasonable constraints for management and conservation purposes.
Acceptance by visitors of the needs of land management, and understanding of how this sustains the livelihood, culture

and community interests of those who live and work in the hills.

Acceptance by land managers of the public's expectation of having access to the hills.

Acknowledgment of a common interest in the natural beauty and special qualities of Scotland's hills, and the need to work together for their protection and enhancement.

The Forum point out that the success of the Concordat will depend on all who manage or visit the hills acting on these four principles. In addition, the parties to the Concordat will promote good practice in the form of:

Courtesy and consideration at a personal level.

A welcome to visitors.

Making advice readily available on the ground or in advance.

Better information about the uplands and hill land uses through environmental education.

Respect by visitors for the welfare needs of livestock and wildlife.

Adherence to relevant codes and standards of good practice by visitors and land managers alike.

An Cabar in Ben Wyvis National Nature Reserve

Any local restrictions on access should be essential for the needs of management, should be fully explained, and be for the minimum period and area required.

Queries should be addressed to:
Access Forum Secretariat, c/o Recreation and Access Branch, Scottish Natural Heritage, 2 Anderson Place, Edinburgh EH6 5NP.

Safety on the Hills

The Highland hills and lower but remote areas call for care and respect. The idyllic landscape of the tourist brochures can change rapidly into a world of gales, rain and mist, potentially lethal for those ill-equipped or lacking navigational skills. The Scottish hills in winter can be arctic in severity, and even in summer, snow can lash the summits. It is essential that the walker is aware of these hazards, which are discussed more fully in the introduction (see page 14).

At the very least carry adequate wind- and waterproof outer garments, food and drink to spare, a basic first-aid kit, whistle, map and compass – and know how to use them. Wear boots. Plan within your capabilities. If going alone, ensure that you leave details of your proposed route.

Heed local advice, listen to weather forecasts, and do not hesitate to modify plans if conditions deteriorate.

Some of the walks in this book (especially walks 23 to 28) venture into remote country and others climb high summits, and these expeditions should only be undertaken in good summer conditions. In winter they could well need the skills and experience of mountaineering rather than walking. In midwinter the hours of daylight are of course much curtailed, but given crisp, clear late-winter days many of the shorter expeditions would be perfectly feasible, if the guidelines given are adhered to. THINK is the only actual rule. Your life may depend on that. Seek to learn more

Glossary of Gaelic Names

Most of the place-names in this region are Gaelic in origin, and this list gives some of the more common elements, which will allow readers to understand otherwise meaningless words and appreciate the relationship between place-names and landscape features. Place-names often have variant spellings, and the more common of these are given here.

aber	mouth of loch, river	eilidh	hind
abhainn	river	eòin, eun	bird
allt	stream	fionn	white
auch, ach	field	fraoch	heather
bal, bail, baile	town, homestead	gabhar, ghabhar,	
bàn	white, fair, pale	gobhar	goat
bealach	hill pass	garbh	rough
beg, beag	small	geal	white
ben, beinn	hill	ghlas, glas	grey
bhuidhe	yellow	gleann, glen	narrow, valley
blar	plain	gorm	blue, green
brae, braigh	upper slope, steepening	inbhir, inver	confluence
		inch, inis, innis	island, meadow by
breac	speckled		river
cairn	pile of stones, often marking a summit	lag, laggan	hollow
		làrach	old site
cam	crooked	làirig	pass
càrn	cairn, cairn-shaped hill	leac	slab
		liath	grey
caol, kyle	strait	loch	lake
ceann, ken, kin	head	lochan	small loch
cil, kil	church, cell	màm	pass, rise
clach	stone	maol	bald-shaped top
clachan	small village	monadh	upland, moor
cnoc	hill, knoll, knock	mór, mor(e)	big
coille, killie	wood	odhar, odhair	dun-coloured
corrie, coire,		rhu, rubha	point
choire	mountain hollow	ruadh	red, brown
craig, creag	cliff, crag	sgòr, sgòrr,	
crannog,		sgùrr	pointed
crannag	man-made island	sron	nose
dàl, dail	field, flat	stob	pointed
damh	stag	strath	valley (broader than
dearg	red		glen)
druim, drum	long ridge	tarsuinn	traverse, across
dubh, dhu	black, dark	tom	hillock (rounded)
dùn	hill fort	tòrr	hillock (more rugged)
eas	waterfall	tulloch, tulach	knoll
ellean	island	uisge	water, river

about the Highlands and your part in them, and continue to develop your skills and broaden your experience.

Mountain Rescue

In case of emergency the standard procedure is to dial 999 and ask for the police who will assess and deal with the situation.

First, however, render first aid as required and make sure the casualty is made warm and comfortable. The distress signal (six flashes/whistle-blasts, repeated at minute intervals) may bring help from other walkers in the area. Write down essential details: exact location (six-figure reference), time of accident, numbers involved, details of injuries, steps already taken; then despatch a messenger to phone the police.

If leaving the casualty alone, mark the site with an eye-catching object. Be patient; waiting for help can seem interminable.

Useful Organisations

Association for the Protection of Rural Scotland
Gladstone's Land, 3rd floor
483 Lawnmarket, Edinburgh EH1 2NT
Tel. 0131 225 7012

Forestry Commission
Information Department
231 Corstorphine Road
Edinburgh EH12 7AT
Tel. 0131 334 0303

Historic Scotland
Longmore House, Salisbury Place,
Edinburgh EH9 1SH
Tel. 0131 668 8600

Long Distance Walkers' Association
21 Upcroft, Windsor, Berkshire SL4 3NH
Tel. 01753 866685

National Trust for Scotland
5 Charlotte Square, Edinburgh EH2 4DU
Tel. 0131 226 5922

Ordnance Survey
Romsey Road, Southampton SO16 4GU
Tel. 08456 05 05 05 (Lo-call)

Ramblers' Association (main office)
1/5 Wandsworth Road, London SW8 2XX
Tel. 0171 582 6878

Ramblers' Association (Scotland)
23 Crusader House, Haig Business Park,
Markinch, Fife KY7 6AQ
Tel. 01592 611177

Royal Society for the Protection of Birds
North Scotland Regional Office
Etive House, Beechwood Park
Inverness IV2 3BW
Tel. 01463 715000

Scottish Natural Heritage
12 Hope Terrace
Edinburgh EH9 2AS
Tel. 0131 447 4784

Scottish Rights of Way Society Ltd
John Cotton Business Centre,
10 Sunnyside
Edinburgh EH7 5RA
Tel. 0131 652 2937

Scottish Wildlife Trust
Cramond House, Kirk Cramond
Cramond Glebe Road
Edinburgh EH4 6NS
Tel. 0131 312 7765

Scottish Youth Hostels Association
7 Glebe Crescent, Stirling FK8 2JA
Tel. 01786 451181

Tourist Information
Scottish Tourist Board
23 Ravelston Terrace
Edinburgh EH4 3EU
Tel. 0131 332 2433

Local tourist information offices:
Dornoch: 01862 810490
Dufftown: 01340 820501 (Apr-Nov)
Elgin: 01343 542666
Forres: 01309 672938 (Apr-Nov)
Fort Augustus: 01320 366367 (Apr-Oct)

Helmsdale: 01431 821640 (late Mar-Sep)
Inverness: 01463 234353
John o'Groats: 01955 611373 (Apr-Oct)
Nairn: 01667 452753 (Apr-Oct)
North Kessock: 01463 731505
Strathpeffer: 01997 421415 (Apr-Nov)
Wick: 01955 602596

Weather Forecasts
Mountaincall East Tel. 0891 500442
Scotland seven-day forecast
Tel. 0891 112260
UK seven-day forecast Tel. 0891 333123

Ordnance Survey Maps of Inverness, Loch Ness and the North East Highlands

Inverness, Loch Ness and the North East Highlands are covered by Ordnance Survey 1:50 000 scale (1¼ inches to 1 mile or 2cm to 1km) Landranger map sheets 7, 10, 12, 16, 17, 20, 21, 25, 26, 27, 28, 29, 33, 34, 35. These all-purpose maps are packed with information to help you explore the area – viewpoints, picnic sites, places of interest and caravan and camping sites are all shown.

To examine Inverness, Loch Ness and the North East Highlands in more detail, the following Pathfinder maps at 1:25 000 scale (2½ inches to 1 mile or 4cm to 1km) cover the area:

41 (ND37/47)	145 (NH96/NJ06)
58 (ND25/35)	146 (NJ16/26)
65 (NC84/94)	147 (NJ36/46)
74 (NC 43/53)	159 (NH45/55)
76 (NC83/93)	160 (NH65/75)
77 (ND03/13)	161 (NH85/95)
84 (NC42/52)	162 (NJ05/15)
87 (ND02/12)	163 (NJ25/35)
96 (NC81/91)	177 (NH64/74)
106 (NC80/90)	196 (NJ23/33)
113 (NH49/59)	206 (NH02/12)
115 (NH79/89)	207 (NH22/32)
123 (NH68/78)	208 (NH42/52)
124 (NH88/98)	238 (NH20/30)
143 (NH46/56)	251 (NN29/39)
144 (NH 66/76)	252 (NN49/59)

To get to the area use the Ordnance Survey Great Britain Routeplanner (Travelmaster map 1) at 1:625 000 scale (1 inch to 10 miles or 1cm to 6.25km) or Travelmaster map 2 (Northern Scotland, Orkney and Shetland) at 1:250 000 scale (1 inch to 4 miles or 1 cm to 2.5km).

Ordnance Survey maps and guides are available from most booksellers, stationers and newsagents.

The view west along Loch Affric

Index

Entries in italics refer to illustrations